This small book is dedicated to Charles Brett (my grandfather), murdered by incompetent officers, and to my grandchildren, so that they will know where they come from.

Charlie

&

Bluebell Hill Boy

Two biographical sketches

by

Colin Brett

Charlie & Bluebell Hill Boy
Two biographical sketches

Colin Brett

Published by

LOAF ON A STICK PRESS

Nottingham, November 2016

For more information please see

People's Histreh
Nottingham & Notts Radical History Group

http://peopleshistreh.wordpress.com
http://twitter.com/PeoplesHistreh
peopleshistreh@riseup.net

ISBN 9780956913999

Printed by
ImprintDigital.com, Devon

Contents

Illustrations

The cover image shows British infantry at Loos, advancing through the gas cloud on the 25th September 1915. It is superimposed with a photograph of Charlie's name on the Loos Memorial, taken by Colin Brett during a visit to France.

Acknowledgements

First to Claire and Mike for pointing me to the folk who put this book together for me.

Also to Dave Hewitt, a good comrade of mine, who on reading my two stories gave me lots of encouragement.

Last but not least to Philipp who not only painstakingly edited my stories, but offered me many suggestions, tips, etc.

Without him this book would not be.

Editors' note:

We also thank PICTURE THE PAST *and of course Tawina, Ruth and our other test readers for all their work and invaluable feedback.*

But most of all we want to thank Colin for his work and for his patience whilst we were getting our act together.

Foreword

By People's Histreh[1]

If you previously picked up one of our books or attended one of our events, thanks a lot and welcome back. If this is the first time you have encountered us, many thanks and welcome to you too!

We are a Nottingham based group, united by a passion for history from below (people's history, grassroots history – or whatever you want to call it). Although this description implies a certain degree of organisation and professionalism, do not be fooled, we are simply a bunch of people who occasionally meet for cake and chats about awesome documents. Sometimes this will result in a talk or guided walk, and every now and then in the publication of a pamphlet or a proper book.

Over the past seven years we have looked into various subjects, be it local grass-roots organisation of Chartists and Co-operators, the so-called 'Reform Riots' (during which our Castle went up in flames), or the 'Great Cheese Riot' of 1766 (an intriguing subject even if you do not share an enthusiasm for cheese).

Doing so, we have focussed on the so-called 'ordinary' people, whose lives, labours and struggles have shaped the world around us. Even though the historians' trade has changed a lot for the better over

---

1 For more information on *People's Histreh – Nottingham and Notts Radical History Group*, as well as news, updates and numerous free downloads, please see our blog: http://peopleshistreh.wordpress.com

past decades, these people still get side-lined far too often for a history focussing on the ruling classes, reducing everyone else to an amorphous mass that every so often congeals into a (riotous, patriotic, etc.) 'mob', depicting most people as being swept along by, rather than making their own, history.

We have always tried to spot faces in the crowds, and strived to give some of these people their voices back, exemplified for instance by the work of our very own Chris Richardson, who has painstakingly retraced the stories of many incredible people whose lives and deeds had been all but forgotten.[2]

We have however never before ventured out of the comfortable realm of non-fiction. And we would have probably kept it that way had it not been for our friend and comrade Colin,[3] approaching us with the manuscript of a story about his grandad, who had been killed in World War One. Originally written over a decade ago, Colin received an offer to get this work published, but was quick to decline that publisher's condition that he could not call the officers who had sent his grandad to his death 'murderers'.

It should be no surprise that this got our attention.

---

2 See RICHARDSON, CHRISTOPHER: *A City of Light - Socialism, Chartism and Co-operation – Nottingham 1844*; Loaf On A Stick Press; 2nd edition Nottingham 2015.

3 Many locals will recognise Colin's characteristic hat, surrounded by an ever-present cloud of fag-smoke, from many struggles fought in the last decades, notably against the Poll Tax in the late 1980s and early 1990s. This most reliable comrade can still be found up front at any anti-fascist action.

Colin's story is a fictionalised biographical sketch of the final year of his grandad's life. Based on a number of primary sources,[4] it follows the story of some 'ordinary' folks caught up in the brutal mess that was World War One.

By writing this story, Colin has made his own contribution to the ongoing remembrance of World War One. This conflict continues to cast a very long shadow over British society and remains the subject of many controversies, which by now have quite a history themselves.

Within a couple of decades after the armistice, many libraries had already been filled with artistic and historic takes on the events which continue to be seen as bringing cataclysmic changes, marking the end of the long nineteenth century, and heralding the beginning of an *Age of Extremes*.[5]

Even before the guns fell silent on the Western Front, many tales were spun of a valiant Empire, coming together in a great though terrible struggle.

---

4 Although he used a number of original sources to write his story, Colin has taken some artistic license, especially regarding his family's history. His depiction of Charlie's family life in 1914 is for instance based on Charlie's first marriage, which ended when Eliza Brett died in 1902. In 1909 Charlie married Mary Warren. Albert, Colin's father, was the youngest child of Charlie and Eliza. Mary's and Charlie's only child Maud was born in 1910. Some eagle eyed readers (especially those who have studied the Battle of Loos) might spot a number of other details which are not quite historically accurate.

5 See e.g.: HOBSBAWM, ERIC: *The Age of Revolution*; idem: *The Age of Capital 1848-1875*; idem: *The Age of Empire*; idem: *The Age of Extremes 1914-1991*.

Numerous works perpetuated these myths, for example many of the proud battalion histories, often written by former officers in the late 1910s and 1920s and usually lacking any wider historic or explicitly political angle. It did however not take long for the 'war poets' and many others to attempt to deal with the incomprehensible physical and psychological traumas of combatants and non-combatants in rather different and much more critical ways.

As the events became more remote, disputes on how to interpret them did not lose any of their fervour. If anything, the controversies became more heated from the 1960s, for instance following the publication of Alan Clark's (in-)famous work *The Donkeys*, which became an inspiration to many and further popularised an interpretation of World War One as the epitome of pointless mass-slaughter.

To this day an understanding of the war as a futile slugging match, during which incompetent fools ordered brave heroes time and again to achieve the impossible, remains firmly anchored in the wider public conscience.

In more recent years this has been challenged to some extent by a wave of new revisionists, historians like Gary Sheffield, whose ideas have also been picked up in many recent populist portrayals of the conflict. These new revisionists have put in a lot of effort to restore the Donkeys' reputation. They portray the war not so much as one bloody disaster after another, but as a long (i.e. rather flat) learning curve, culminating in

1918 in the ascent of a modern form of the legitimised mass murder that is warfare.[6]

What the new revisionists did, often in meticulous work with previously unreleased, unknown or neglected sources, was not without merit. They do indeed have a point stating that Clark and others had worked rather sloppily in places and that commonly held views of key persons and events do not account for the complexity evident in the primary sources. The new revisionists' work does however not only have many rather despicable political implications,[7] and repeatedly crosses the line to servile admiration for people whom we will always describe as mass murderers, it also tends to neglect the experiences of individuals not wearing brass hats.

---

6 One strand of the new revisionists' arguments has been that military commanders, especially 'Butcher' Haig, rather than being a bunch of blockheads hopelessly stuck in the long nineteenth century, were in fact open to new ideas on how to come to terms with the realities of industrialised warfare on an unprecedented scale. These historians conclude that military commanders had to "experiment", to gradually figure out how (not) to fight such a war. Books like SHEFFIELD'S *Forgotten Victory*… are prime examples of this strand of World War One historiography, describing how after each bloody blunder, or, in his words, "mishandled" battles, the British Army was "absorbing the perceived lessons of the fighting", whilst there was "a healthy interest in innovation and experimentation at all levels" (SHE; p110). All those lessons meant that the British Army became, after only four years of slaughter, something the new revisionists portray as a formidable, proto-World War Two, fighting machine, with new (tanks, aeroplanes) and older (infantry, artillery) branches of the military working together efficiently, finally beating the Germans after the offensives of summer and autumn 1918.

7 See for instance Michael Gove's ramblings on the subject.

It has been said that once the blood has dried, revisionism can creep in[8] and it seems that this has happened indeed. Many of the more recent publications on World War One are far less influenced by the immediacy of terror which had so strongly influenced earlier writers who experienced the war at first hand.

This is hardly surprising, given that the war has moved beyond the realm of living history. Those killed in the conflict are long gone. The survivors, mutilated to varying degrees in body and soul, are dead, as are their parents, partners and most of their children.

Although remembrance of the war continues to be mostly heartfelt and sincere, the deep wounds in the collective psyche are no longer raw. When we remember the war today we usually venerate anonymous symbols and often do so in highly ritualised ways, such as poppies streaming out of palaces or child-soldiers giving salutes in front of stone memorials.[9]

Although many people do remember individuals (genealogy has become a thriving industry), these

---

8 The term historical revisionism has very negative connotations and is often used as a slur against those pushing a conservative interpretation of history. There are numerous despicable examples of historical revisionism, such as Ernst Nolte's attempt to portray the crimes of German fascism as a reaction to events in the Soviet Union. We also use the term in a negative sense, but are aware that revisionism per se is simply the process of challenging established ideas about a subject, and therefore lies at the basis of sound historic work.

9 Seeing children in Army Cadet Force uniforms performing militarist rituals at memorials and gravesites remains a spine-chilling sight.

individuals often remain silent. There are of course many sources which record contemporaries' experiences and these can partly bridge the widening gulf between us and them. However, as we search for specific individuals, much of the time we must consider ourselves lucky to find a few records routinely left by army and civilian administrations. Most of these sources reduce peoples' lives to a bit of data in lists and tables, offering only indirect traces of the complex experiences that combatants and non-combatants lived through. It usually takes quite a bit of luck and patience to reconstruct a version of what they may have experienced, a task much complicated by the inescapable problem that we can only ever ask, explore and 'understand' the past through the prism of our own perceptions of the present.

At the moment we are ourselves confronted with the challenges of how to reconstruct some of the experiences of people who lived through the war. Since 2014 we have been immersed in a research project, looking into the stories of soldiers who served in the local regiment between 1914 and 1918 and were sentenced to death or court martialled following their alleged involvement in mutinies.

In undertaking this research and putting together our interpretation of the events we try to work as meticulously as possible. Radical history projects have too often discredited themselves by making shallow or unfounded arguments, giving in to the temptation of telling tales of ruthless villains and revolutionary heroines and heroes. But we also have no intention of trying to distil a pseudo-objective account from the available evidence.

Instead, one thing that drives our work is anger and we feel it imperative to keep that anger alive, regardless of how much time has passed. We remain angry with those sending millions to their deaths and angry with all those working class people who allowed themselves to be fooled by all the waffle about Kings, Kaisers, fatherlands and other follies, rather than to engage in acts of anti-national solidarity.[10]

Reading *Charlie*, there is no doubt that Colin also continues to be very angry about what happened to his grandad. Indeed, on many levels Colin did what we strive to do, he just went down a very different route. To understand something about and to remember a man he could very much relate to, but never had a chance to meet, Colin decided to write his story about Charlie, for himself, for his family and for all of us.

Colin's solidarity with his characters is obvious, but he never glorifies them. Charlie and his mates make mistakes, are led astray by a mix of economic and propagandist pressures, and end up well over their heads in a terrifying mess, desperately hoping to get out in one piece.

Never trying to hide his politics, Colin leaves us in no doubt where the real enemy needs to be fought:

---

10 As we continue to look back in anger, we hope against hope to one day live in a world where we do no longer have to be angry about the present.

not across the other side of no-man's-land, but behind their own lines.

Our comrade wrote a story about his family, exploring his own history by imagining some of the experiences of working-class folks like himself, creating a remarkable account of some 'ordinary' people living through extraordinary times.

We opted to place *Charlie* between this (bloated) introduction and another chapter written by us, looking into the wider and the specific context of Charlie's battle. This is followed by Colin's second story, an autobiographical text about the world he grew up in.

Recounting his life and childhood adventures in and around the terraces of St Ann's, *Bluebell Hill Boy* allows us to glimpse into the everyday experiences of a very young Colin, a Nottingham working class lad whose life was shaped by two World Wars, massive social and economic changes as well as ever accelerating technological progress.

Bluebell Hill Boy almost reads like an oral history interview and is an important document about a world and a culture that has itself become part of our history – indeed this is the very stuff social history is made of!

Working with Colin to make his stories available to others has been a privilege and we thank him very much for entrusting us with his manuscripts.[11]

---

[11] Publishing something other than a work of strict non-fiction will however almost certainly remain a one-off.

We can only hope that you not only have a good read, but that you might feel inspired to follow Colin's example and explore your own history to get a better idea of what made your world the way it is – and what it might become.

Valentine Yarnspinner

October 2016

Charlie

One man's battle at Loos, France 1915

Glossary

We have been trying to avoid too many army-isms, but the following might nevertheless be useful:

BATTALION	A formation of soldiers, at full strength comprising around 1,000 persons. Although further subdivided (into COMPANIES etc.), a BATTALION was the smallest building block of larger troop formations. It was also the smallest unit in the British Army to produce its own admin, for example the so-called battalion *War Diaries.*
BEF	BRITISH EXPEDITIONARY FORCE: the official designation of the forces drawn from all over the British Empire and sent to the Western Front.
BRIGADE	A formation of soldiers usually made up of four, at later stages of the war three, BATTALIONS.
DIVISION	A formation of soldiers made up of three or four BRIGADES, as well as artillery, engineer and medical units.
CORPS	A formation of soldiers consisting of several DIVISIONS. This rung in the chain of command had mostly strategic and administrative functions, although some units were permanently allocated to certain CORPS, for example heavy artillery batteries.
HUNS	Derogatory slang term for Germans, widely used by British troops.
NCO	NON-COMMISSIONED OFFICER: low ranking officers (corporals, sergeants, etc.). Other than commissioned officers NCOs usually came from the same social and economic backgrounds as most PRIVATES (the lowest and thus most common military rank).
RSM	REGIMENTAL SERGEANT MAJOR, a senior NCO.

Preface

Whilst investigating my family genealogy, it was discovered that one of my ancestors, my grandad Charlie, was killed in World War One. Curiosity led me in 2006 to visit the area in which he died. Back home I felt closer to this man whom I never knew, yet somehow felt I wanted to know him more.

So I wrote this small story. It worked for me, and Charlie has become more alive, and is no longer just a name in a book.

I hope it does the same for you.

Home

Charlie slipped and slithered his way down Drury Hill. He was wet through on this dark, dank November night. The snow had started to turn to a slippery slush, and the drizzly rain was just about to turn to ice as it hit the cobblestones on this steep narrow thoroughfare.

Finally skidding his way to the bottom, he sighed. "Not far to go now" he muttered to himself. So through the narrow dirty hovel of streets in Narrow Marsh he wended his way home with back bent against the stinging sleet until finally he arrived at Lomas yard.

This squalid yard was like most others in this poor working class area in the south of Nottingham. Built in their thousands by jerry-builders to house the lace workers of the district. Some said there were as many pubs as dwellings.

Lomas yard consisted of twenty to thirty rabbit hutches that folk called houses, all formed in a square and entered by what was called a twitchel. Five toilets stood ragged in the centre of this square, and two water standpipes at either end furnished this ugly scene. Hardly any bright daylight or sunshine penetrated this dreary yard, for so closely packed were they built. No air circulated and the acrid smell of toilets and rotting vegetables hung in the air.

"Jesus Christ!" uttered Elsie as Charlie got indoors. "You will catch your death of cold, get them wet clothes off and put em near the fire." Ten minutes later, with dry clothes on and his wet ones steaming on the hob at the side of the fireplace, Charlie said: "What's for dinner lass?" "Irish stew," she replied. "Ah good" he thought, "I like Irish stew, warms you up on a night like this."

Elsie returned from the small scullery with a piping hot basin of stew and thick chunks of bread. He wolfed it down in record time, and then asked, "Any more love?" Picking up his empty basin she was soon back with his second helping. But this time it was only half full and no bread. After finishing that off, he retrieved his pipe from the high mantelpiece, and lit up with some St Bruno.

"Any luck today Charlie?" she enquired. "No, sod all, me and George Winterbottom been all up Mapperley Top, Sneinton, Woodborough and the Park. Nothing doing. Chance maybe in two months' time on some new houses going up, but nowt definite." He and George Winterbottom (all his mates called him cold arse) were slaters labourers. Yet this time of winter in 1914 nobody needed them. Charlie himself had been out of work for over eight weeks, yet things were not as bleak for him and his family as others in the district. At least Elsie was thrifty when it came to money. She knew where every penny went and exactly how much money was in her purse. What with some ironing she did for some rich family in the Park three days a week, they were not destitute. Not yet anyway.

Charlie moved closer to the fire, his hands outstretched, only inches away from the glowing embers. "Where's our Albert?" "Over at the Wilson's of twenty-two, I told him to be back by four. I'll bat his tab when he gets in, it's nearly five o'clock now," retorted Elsie, as she washed a few pots in the scullery sink. "Aw leave him be." replied Charlie. "Lads of thirteen have no idea about time. They think five minutes is five hours." Elsie sighed. "You're too soft Charlie Brett, too soft. You're a good man our Charlie but you're too soft." She returned to the small room, wiping her hands on her apron.

"Hey wake up Ada, wake up dear or you won't sleep tonight." Elsie had just walked over to the small two seater dilapidated settee. Little Ada was only four. She rubbed her eyes and sat up. "Your dad's home Ada, your dad's home." Charlie's other sons and daughters lived elsewhere, but not too far away. "Aye up duck, give your dad a kiss." Ada smiled. "Gorrany chocolate dad?" Charlie picked her up. "Not today sweetheart, but I promise to get you some tomorrow." Her face dropped. "Then I won't kiss you." He laughed as he put her down saying. "Cheeky little blighter, nobody will mess her about when she grows up that's for sure."

The front door slammed shut as young Albert entered. He tried to duck but Elsie caught him one good wallop on the ear. "Four o'clock means four o'clock young man, sit down, shut up and get this down yer." Elsie produced young Albert's steaming basin of stew and chunks of bread. Looking up from his meal, his eyes caught his dad looking at him. Albert smiled and Charlie winked back at him, and then returned to read his *Nottingham Evening Post.*

"Hey Elsie, listen to this. Over eight thousand from Nottingham have signed up since August." Elsie frowned. "Yes, eight thousand fools more like. You men are all the same, you all just love fighting. It's time us women had a say in running the country. We couldn't do any worse than your lot. Anyway, I've more serious things to think about, like where's next week's rent coming from? And I owe Jenkins the butcher a few bob, and the coalman wants paying tomorrow or we don't get no more. So don't talk to me about war."

Charlie realised he had touched on a sore point with Elsie, so shut up and got on with reading his paper. The damp darkness set in, and by eight o'clock both Albert and Ada were in the land of nod upstairs, with a hot plate shelf from the fireside hob and some old overcoats on the bed for extra warmth. Charlie stood up and turned his back to the fireplace warming his backside. Taking out his watch from his waistcoat pocket, he wound it up and turned it over. It was the only good possession he had, silver it was on a silver chain. A gift from his father Nicholas Brett, who told Charlie it was given to him by his father, also named Nicholas. Charlie had heard many times before the story of how his grandfather, wife Catherine, and their four sons had left Ireland in about 1847 and settled down in Nottingham. No doubt, thought Charlie, because of the famine.

"I'll give this watch to young Albert when he gets a bit older." "If you give it to him now," chuckled Elsie, "he won't get no more clips round the earhole." Both laughed.

Charlie thought: "Elsie's in a good mood. So here goes." He approached her. "Err Elsie love, any chance of a few coppers, I could murder a pint?" Now Charlie wasn't what you might call a boozer, but liked the odd pint or two now and again. Without a word she reached for an old tea tin on the mantelpiece, fumbled about in it, then gave him a few coins. "There, and don't be too late, I've got to be up early tomorrow, have to be at the Browns in the Park for seven." He pocketed the money. "Ta love, give us a kiss." Elsie stepped back. "Geroff with you and don't be late."

The Dirty Duck was only half full as Charlie got his pint, looked round, and espied George, Mick and Malky sitting in the corner. He ambled over, nodded and sat down. "Aye Up Charlie lad, any luck today?" "Not a sausage." replied Charlie sipping at his beer. "And you know why?" It was George. "Because all tax money is going to fight this bloody war, that's what." Charlie snapped back instantly. "But somebody's got to stop the Germans, or they will be coming over Trent Bridge and knocking on your door Georgy boy and you won't like that boyo." George shifted in his chair but said nothing. Malky now chipped in. "Charlie, heard about the bakers up the road, no? Well I'll tell you. All the staff, manager included have all signed up yesterday. All twenty-three of em, lock, stock and barrel." Charlie sat bolt upright. "Never."

"Yep the whole lot of em. Smart looking recruiting sergeant came down from the Sherwood Foresters. Gave them all a lecture for about half an hour. He then handed out forms, and the bloody lot signed up. They go to training camp in Derbyshire next week." Charlie was taken aback at this news. "Well I never." he gasped. "Why old Bill Drummond must be fifty if he's a day." Malky nodded. "Yes I know, but even he signed on the dotted line. Told em he was much younger. The army don't care how old or young you are nowadays, so long as you can walk, you're in."

The cold evening passed by, and Charlie with three pints in him bid goodnight to one and all. A flurry of snow drifted into the pub as Charlie opened the door to leave. "See you Charlie, don't do ote I wouldn't do." It was freezing outside as he navigated his way home. Once indoors, he headed straight for bed. All was quiet, and Elsie was fast asleep.

November passed and December came in with a snowstorm. One day, December the 8th to be exact,

Charlie returned home at two o'clock after being out all morning. He hung his cap on a nail in the scullery door, ruffled Albert's hair, sat down and looked very seriously at Elsie. "What's up, what you looking at me like that for, what you done, are you in trouble?" Charlie, feeling uneasy replied: "No duck nowt of the sort. Elsie dear, sit down, I've got summat to tell you." Elsie nervously wiped her hands on her apron, and sat down. "Is it our Ethel, I know she's none too good?" Albert was curious and came nearer. "No Elsie it's not about Ethel, don't get mad, but I… I… I've been and signed up." Elsie flew out of the chair, and both Charlie and Albert jumped back in surprise. "What?" screamed Elsie at the top of her voice. The whole yard must have heard it. "What, you stupid man, look at you, you're forty-one for god's sake not twenty-one. What in god's name made you go and do it?" she made her way to a picture on the wall of the Virgin Mary. Crossing herself saying: "Mary, Mary mother of god, help us, help us." Then collapsing back to the chair she burst out sobbing. Young Albert rushed to her side, and he too started crying.

Charlie paced the floor up and down. "Look Elsie, we're always skint every bloody week, Albert here needs some shoes, and Ada lives in hand-me-downs. At least you'll get regular money each week, the officer told me." Elsie frowned at him. "Yes, and get yourself bloody killed. What do we do then, go begging like the Ramsdens at number four?" Charlie approached her. "Don't talk daft Elsie duck, I won't see the front line at my age anyway. Besides, do you know that for every soldier with a rifle in his hand at the front, there's plenty of others needed to back him up and keep him there? There's drivers, cooks and medics, plus a lot more besides."

Between sobs she stuttered "You won't come back Charlie, I know it, you won't come back." Elsie looked at red-eyed Albert. "Go fetch your sister from your auntie's, it's time for her tea. Go on now there's a good lad, I'm alright." Albert looked at his dad. "Go on son, do as she says."

Now alone, Charlie got on bended knee in front of Elsie and placed one hand on her shoulder. "Look duck, it will probably all be over in a few months' time, you wait and see. Elsie dear, I don't feel like a real man anymore, no work, and having to ask you for the odd bob or two. It aint right. Bill and Wally have joined up too." Fiddling with her apron strings, she moaned. "Yes, but Bill and Wally aint got no wife or kids to keep." Charlie in desperation stood up pacing up and down again. "I know, but look at us Elsie. Come on, have a good look round. The furniture is all falling to pieces, we owe money here and there, and everything we got is crap and second hand. At least from now on you'll get my regular money coming in each week." Still not looking at him she said amidst sobs: "I don't want regular money Charlie, I want you at home with me and the kids. Don't go Charlie, I beg of you, don't go." Charlie was getting fed up the way it was going. He took a deep breath: "Too late Elsie, too late. I've been and gone and done it, that's the end of it, can't back out now. I leave for Derby Saturday, probably get some home leave after a few weeks training."

After a dinner eaten in silence, she donned hat and coat, saying: "I'm off to tell the family what a stupid daft man I married." She slammed the door hard shut.

Away

20652 Private Brett, Charles, 12th Battalion Sherwood Foresters, was on home leave. It was August 1915. Elsie by now had resigned herself to the fact that her man was in "this bloody war" as she told people.

Over the long lonely months, she had read and seen many photos of the soldiers killed in action or dying from their wounds in the *Evening Post.* She had also read all about how a battle near a Belgium town called Ypres had been yet another complete success with over 34,000 Germans killed, wounded or missing. Elsie was not stupid or naïve, and wondered why, if the papers were correct that the Germans lost every battle, why was this war still carrying on?

"It's insane," she muttered out loud. "The world's gone stark raving loony mad." Young Albert was showing off his dad's cap to the lads in the yard. Ordinary boys' games like snobs, conkers and marbles had gone out of the window. Now it was war games in the hovels of Narrow Marsh.

"Bang, bang! You're dead!"

"No I'm not, you missed me."

"You dirty German pig, bang, bang!"

"I'm not playing, I always have to be a German, it's not fair."

"Well at least" Elsie thought, "Charlie does look well on army life." He had put on some much needed weight, having been only nine stone when he went for his army medical, and she had to admit to herself that the small bit of army money each week had at least been handy. "But at what price," she thought, "at what price?" Another thing she had to admit to herself was, she really felt proud as she and Charlie walked down the street together, him looking so smart in his uniform.

The last night of Charlie's leave, he took her to a few of the pubs in the district. He bade farewell to many of his friends and relations. He was about to be sent to Chobham Common camp in Surrey, just north of Woking. Rumour had it that his battalion would soon be on their way over the sea, to Flanders or northern France.

Charlie and the rest of his battalion hadn't yet seen, let alone handled a real rifle. It had been ages before they had even got uniforms, wearing their own clothes whilst using wooden imitations for guns on endless the marches and parades. After they did finally get uniforms, caps with shiny badges and all, it was more marching and parades, with a lot of time spent polishing belt buckles, and all the time dig, dig, dig and dig more. Yes digging was their game, for the 12th Battalion Sherwood Foresters was a pioneer outfit, the armed builders and labourers of the British Army. "Any digging wants doing, any heavy unloading? Yes my men will do it, it's their job."

Within a fortnight from leaving home once more, Charlie, along with Bill and Wally, both also from

Narrow Marsh, were digging a trench about four foot deep. Wally wiped his brow in this hot August sun. "Phew it's fucking hot today Charlie. How would you like to be at Trent Bridge supping a nice pint of cool clear bitter with your better half and kids?".

"Shurrup Wally!" yelled Charlie. "It only makes it worse if you think of things like that, put it out of your mind." From about ten yards away a voice shrieked: "Hey, you two idle bastards, yes you two! Get digging and no yapping." It was the duty sergeant standing with his hands on his hips. "Or I'll put you both on a fizzer. No time for chitchat when you get over there. Sniper might get you, yes, so heads down and dig, dig, dig. I'll keep my eye on you two." With back bent, Wally thought: "Bollocks". But dig they did for the rest of the day.

"Trench warfare, trench warfare," moaned Wally as they staggered back to their barracks with blistered hands and aching backs. "We aint seen a rifle yet." chimed in Bill Morrison. "What are we supposed to do when we get over there, run at the Hun with our bloody shovels?" He picked his shovel up and slung it on his bed in disgust. "Damaging army property is a court martial offence young man." piped up Wally, trying to talk like an officer. "Piss off Wally!" was the reply.

The trench warfare training continued for a few more backbreaking days. At last the battalion was moved up to Aldershot on the 26th of August, where they actually did some rifle firing. Charlie and his mates enjoyed this, even though the rifle's kickback bruised their shoulders. "Hold it tighter private, it won't bite you. You won't hit a barn door holding it like that, it's not a woman you know." The firing instructor moved on to chastise someone else.

On the 28th the battalion prepared to embark for Southampton. "Well this is it." remarked Charlie: "This is what we signed up for." Wally looked up from polishing his boots. "Hey Charlie, what's gone wrong? It's not so long ago when the government said it will all be over by Christmas, it's now bloody August 1915." To which Charlie replied: "Yeah I know, but it's stalemate Wally, stalemate."

Charlie couldn't sleep that night, his mind full of events in his past, and many worries about the future. So with pencil and paper he decided to write a last letter to Elsie before departing the land of his birth for the first time:

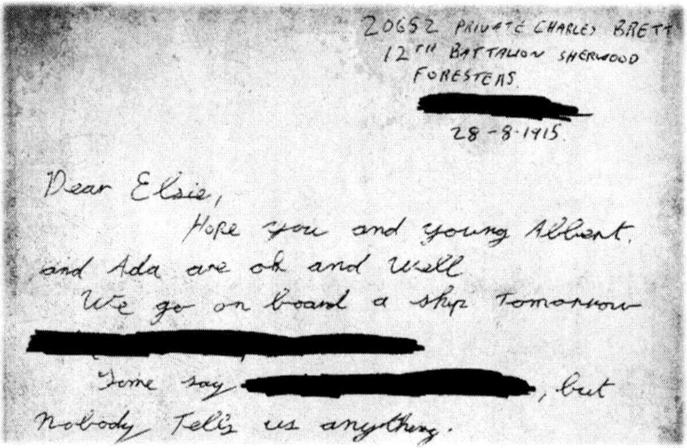
20652 PRIVATE CHARLES BRETT
12TH BATTALION SHERWOOD
FORESTERS
[redacted]
28-8-1915

Dear Elsie,

Hope you and young Albert, and Ada are ok and well
We go on board a ship Tomorrow
[redacted]
Some say [redacted], but nobody Tells us anything.

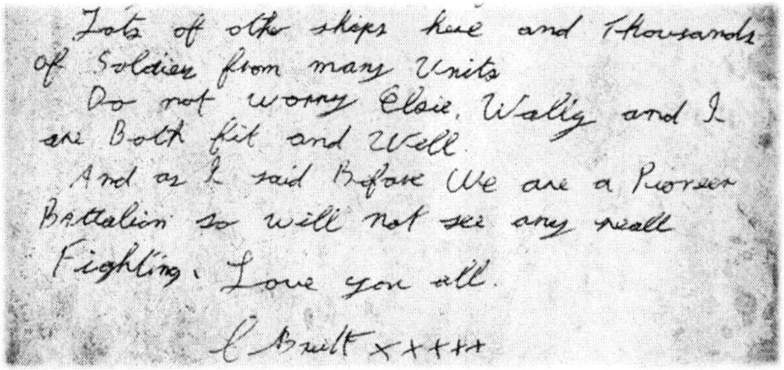
Lots of other ships here and Thousands
of Soldiers from many Units
Do not worry Elsie, Wally and I
are Both fit and Well.
And as I said Before We are a Pioneer
Battalion so will not see any reall
Fighting. Love you all.
C Brett xxxxx

The 12th Battalion arrived at Southampton docks at about 10am on the 29th August, and then had to hang around all day till 5am the following morning for their transport, the *SS Empress Queen*, to Havre in France. It was the first time for some to have seen the sea, although Charlie had once been to Skegness on a day trip with a pubs dart team outing.

"Wow, look at our boat Wally, it's bloody magnificent." Wally stared at this amazing sight. "Must be well over 300 feet long Charlie."

One or two other transport ships were already loading troops abroad, but none of these looked as big and clean as the *Empress Queen.*

Up the gangplank they went. The ship slipped its moorings and silently moved out to sea. No orders were given, so Charlie and Wally drifted around the ship, looking here and there. "Look at this Charlie, and this." They went up and down stairs and along corridors. Although they could see that many furnishings had been taken out when she ship had been refitted as a troop transport, some of what remained was the fanciest they had ever seen in their lives.

It was a calm crossing and most of the lads had stayed up on deck watching England slowly slip out of sight. On reaching Havre on the 30th August, Charlie knelt down and touched French soil. "What did you do that for?" enquired Wally. "Oh just felt like it you know. By the way Wally did you know the beer's crap over here?"

Another voice boomed: "Stop chatting you horrible lot, fall in in threes at the double, that's it. Attention left turn, quick march left, left, left right left..."

March, march, dig, dig

A four-hour march brought them to a woodland place called Camp 2. Nobody told them where they were, but this Camp 2 wasn't too bad at all. Good clean barracks and the hot food were relished by all. The Salvation Army was there and dished out tobacco and sweets to the new arrivals. "Bit like a seaside holiday camp aint it?" said Wally as they settled down for the night. "Yeah I'm sure it is." replied Charlie. "We'll go for a walk on the prom tomorrow, goodnight Wally."

An early but good hot breakfast on the 31st saw them at 8am on the road, marching again for four hours. It was a blistering hot day as they trudged along till finally they arrived at a railway station called Garde-Des-Marchandises. It was a relief for the boys of the 12th to be all seated and let the French railways pull them along. Most took their boots off and relaxed their weary feet.

Charlie saw many thousands of other troops at this station, all going this way and that in a hubbub of activity. A train in a siding was unloading scores of wounded men, French and British. Some were walking wounded and limping, others walked with bandages wrapped round their eyes, each one had a hand on the man in front's shoulder. Then came the victims on stretchers, all heading for horse-drawn carts to take them to army hospitals. Every single one of them looked unkempt and mudded. Wally looked at this very sad and unpleasant sight, and felt a little disturbed. "My God Charlie, look at those poor bastards." Charlie turned to face Wally, and saw that his face had turned to an ashen grey colour. Putting a reassuring arm around Wally's shoulder, Charlie replied: "Now, now Wally, calm down mate. Look, most of them are from proper infantry units. We are pioneers Wally, pioneers." "Yeah I know Charlie, but I don't like the look of things."

"Move on there!" roared the voice of the captain: "We've got a war to fight, at the double now." Wally gathered up his kitbag. "I would like to double him up, right in the middle of his guts," he muttered as he entered the wagons.

Early dawn on this 1st of September saw them pulling into a station named Hesdin after nearly twelve hours on this slow train. Although they had been travelling all night, it had stopped at many places, and shunted into sidings to allow more important cargo to steam by. Trains full of ammunition shells, artillery guns, and trains going back the way they had come. No doubt full of wounded men, thought Charlie. The sun had hardly risen as the 12th detrained. Before long they were on the march again, moving out of Hesdin along narrow country lanes. "Where we going?" moaned Bill. "Nobody tells us owt." "Dunno," answered Charlie. "All I know is that since arriving in France we've been heading in a North Easterly direction."

"Yeah" butted in Wally. "Only snotty nosed officers are allowed maps, and they don't tell you fuck all, all they do is yell at you, do this do that, move this, dig there, it makes you sick." A ten-minute halt was called for, so Charlie and his two mates sat with their backs against a low wall. Black clouds appeared on the horizon in this flat rolling countryside. "Looks like rain Wally." A light drizzle started to fall as they were told to line up again.

Thirty minutes went by, and the troops were getting soaked in this fine rain when moaning Wally was off again: "My legs ache, don't feel they belong to me, wished I had young Tommy Riley's legs over there." Charlie glanced around and espied Tommy about three ranks in front. "Yeah, just look at him. He can't be more than sixteen years old." Bill chipped in. "Talking to him the other day, said he was an orphan from Sneinton, had no job, no money and no kin. Said he joined up this January. I at least get three meals a day now he told me."

They stayed three days in billets at a village called Le-Biez, which were not as good as the first camp billets though. These barns had a number of shutters missing, and badly fitted doors let the draught in. The food was tasteless and lukewarm. Everybody complained, though nothing was done about it. At Le-Biez they trained in fire control, and lectured about discipline, standing orders, and their health. On the third day it chucked it down in buckets, too wet even for the drill sergeant to operate. The boys got a kit inspection, much to their distaste, and Wally was marched off for a haircut escorted by the RSM himself. The lads didn't like this place one bit, so were pleased when on the fourth they were transferred to new billets at Saint-Denœux.

There they were to stay for seventeen days. It was by far the largest site they had yet been to in France. Many other battalions from all sorts of regiments crowded this busy camp.

Charlie and Wally were now transferred to A Company, whilst some others, considered to be good marksmen were sent on special sniper courses. Thinking about all this Charlie wondered why pioneer men went on such courses. He had also heard that officers from the battalion had been going up to the front lines. Doubts slowly began to creep into his mind as to what purpose the higher ups had in mind for the 12th Battalion.

Life was hectic, and the training got heavier and was more intense. Here it was early morning bayonet lessons. The staff sergeant roaring to the lads saying: "I know you all hate me, so think it's me when you stick it in the straw dummy, now charge!" And indeed Wally did. All this plus lots of physical drill to get the boys fit. Yet the officers still found time to squeeze in more digging.

Charlie's company often travelled to Humbert for even more digging and building fortifications. Each evening they wearily returned to Saint-Denœux completely worn out. Wally, like many others, tried to report sick. But the medical officer would have none of it. Even suggesting that a bit more effort and hard work would soon cure him.

"The bastard." retorted Wally. "Look at me hands, I've got more blisters than skin, look. Look!" As Wally showed his hands to all and sundry a distant rumble was heard. "Is that thunder or what?" said Bill, trying to change the subject. "Dunno" answered Charlie, "could be artillery guns, ours or theirs, then again it could be thunder. It's always pissing it down with rain here." Chalky White now put in his pennies worth. "Thought France was a lovely hot place." "No you stupid idiot," it came from private Watson. "That's only at Monte Carlo in the south of France, and that's hundreds of miles away from here. Dint you learn ote at school?"

The days rolled on, and the workload got more intense. Some of the soldiers went to a place called Wizerne, and there did courses on bombing and how to handle smoke canisters. One day smoke helmets were practised, little more than crude sacks soaked in chemicals, maybe protecting them from that devilish poison gas people had been murmuring so much about, but just as much preventing them from breathing at all! Every day saw more bayonet practice, rifle training and extra drill. Intermingled in this seventeen day stay at Saint-Denœux was the good old-fashioned stand by for the 12th, digging and a bit more digging.

At last, on the 21st September, after they got up for their roll call at 6.30am, and had some more rifle and machine gun practice, all the battalion was rounded up. From four o'clock they marched all through the night to Radinghem, via Humbert, St Michel and Monteville.

Nightmare march

It poured it down all night, the narrow country lanes awash with thick sticky mud and deep puddles of water. By now the lads gave up trying to walk by them, and just waded through. Charlie, like the rest of his unit was more than soaked, mud and sludge reached up to his thighs, his eyes smarted from the darting rain, and his belly ached for good hot food. "Keep up lads, won't be long now!" shouted their sergeant. "Soon be in cosy quarters, left right left right, look lively there!" Once more all the battalion thought of one word: "Bollocks."

They finally arrived at Radinghem at half-past three on this cold, wet night. It wasn't as cosy as the sergeant had suggested. Charlie's company were given bivouacs to sleep in. They had seen much use, the bare earth floor was muddy, and past occupants hadn't even bothered to clear up the scores of cigarette ends, soggy paper and empty food containers. A mud stained sock was delicately picked up by Wally and deposited outside at arms-length – as if it was a dead rat with the plague. It was as Bill said: "A god-forsaken hell hole."

Later in the day, most of the lads were complaining amongst themselves about having to work after a gruelling whole night's march in terrible conditions. One barrack room lawyer, Private Brown, was telling everyone that the army regulations stated that after a night's march troops are to be rested the next day for seven hours. "Well fuck off and tell the captain that!"

screamed another. "You're always moaning, trouble with you mate is you moan about this and that, but expect somebody else to fire the bullets for you, your type are all the same. So piss off and see the captain yourself." A rowdy argument followed, and Charlie shook his head and let them get on with it. They were all tired, sodden and hungry, and everybody's temper was on a short fuse.

Charlie lit a damp cigarette, and his thoughts went back to Elsie and the kids at home. The sergeants voice interrupted his thoughts: "Right, fall in you lads, the major wants a word with you."

The officer stood the men at ease and told them: "I am frightfully sorry about the lousy accommodation given to you. Saying that, bad communications were at fault. 12th Battalion wasn't expected here until tomorrow morning, so there's no warm food for the same reason. Again I say sorry, but it's the same for the officers. So we will just have to grin and bear it and manage the best we can. Again I apologise." Wally nudged Charlie. "Well at least this officer doesn't seem too bad a guy, he's said sorry to us three times." The major continued: "Sergeant, keep the troops busy, nothing worse than idle minds. Carry on!" The sergeant saluted: "Sir." He then turned to the men: "Right you heard him, let's get these ammo boxes onto the wagons, come on jump to it!" Wally again nudged Charlie. "I take that back, he's a bastard."

Deep rumblings could now be heard in the distance, and even though it was daylight an occasional flash could be discerned on the far off horizon. It was obvious to one and all that it was not thunder and lightning.

By evening they were back on the road. Passing by a village called Bomy, they were ordered to halt, the road ahead being blocked by some guns which had got stuck. Luckily Charlie and his company had been marching at the rear and were not ordered to join in with the gun crew, having to dig, haul and heave to get the guns moving again. Their mood got even better as they found themselves next to an ammunition cart, and the rather jolly driver invited them to share a smoke.

This was welcome, so Charlie, Wally and a few others sat and rested for a few minutes. Talk now got to other battles and the April Battle of Ypres came up.

"Yeah, we gave the Germans a good hammering there." piped in Wally. "I wouldn't be too sure about that," uttered the driver. "I was behind the lines during that battle and saw many a soldier returning from the fighting. They told me different stories, saying they had seen horrors too terrible to talk about."

Feeling less cheery, they finished their smokes and before long joined the rest of the battalion on their road to god knows where.

Ypres – Five months earlier

Who had been right about the Battle of Ypres? Wally or the driver?

During the spring the Germans had once more tried to take what was left of the Belgian town. Many weeks of fighting saw countless attacks and counter-attacks, which often went like this:

First there came a heavy bombardment, hour upon hour of heavy artillery, from high explosives, howitzers, mortars, and a dozen more variations thrown at the enemy's line. Then a hush fell, which all of a sudden became a screaming whine! Hundreds of whistles were blown, and thousands of men appeared out of the earth like ants leaving the nest. They walked slowly into no-man's-land, that mud infested, crater scarred landscape. The odd one or two dropped, either dead or wounded. Some screamed in agony, others just moaning with pain, whilst some tried to drag their wounded bodies back to the haven of the trench they had just left. Their oncoming buddies just stepped over or around them. They could not stop. Then came that dreaded sound: rat-a-tat-tat, rat-a-tat-tat. The hidden German machine gunners scoured the landscape with countless bullets. Each machine gun capable of firing over a five hundred rounds per minute. They couldn't miss. Hundreds of the British troops fell in this the first fusillade. Those lucky enough not to have been hit stepped up their pace, they stooped and bent their bodies in a futile attempt to make themselves a smaller target. Now the enemy artillery had found their range, and mud, earth and limbs flew up towards the sky, until gravity brought this mangled mess back down to earth. Bits of bloody flesh or skin sometimes landed on a soldier. Many screamed in horror at this, halted, turned and looked back at the way he had come. But always an advancing officer or NCO came up from the rear, roaring: "Turn round lad, keep moving, it's safer moving!" Some of these poor souls even needed a nudge. The trembling trooper turned on wobbly legs, and staggered onwards. Then all of a sudden: Zzip! A neat round hole appeared, middle of his forehead. He dropped, moved no more. He was out of it, and the German sniper looked around for another target.

Rat-a-tat-tat, the music of the German machine gunners echoed around this auditorium of death. The only time they stopped was when the barrel got too hot, but continued their dance of death once cold water had cooled their working parts.

Finally the German wire was reached. A gasp! It was still there. Surely after hours of artillery fire it must have been destroyed. Well that's what they had been told. But no. There it was, still mountains high, and yards in depth. Already scores of dead and dying British were draped on the wire like washing on a line. Still the oncoming rush continued, the barbed wire was cut in some places. Then it was: "Into the trenches lads, kill the bastards." Now the bayonet came into its own. Thrust, parry, jab, twist, pull out, move on, kill, kill, kill. The soldiers screamed as they were taught. When their blades of death went in, skin, bone, muscle and vital organs were ripped and shredded. The Germans threw grenades. The British had no hand grenades back then, so filled empty food cans with explosives and a crude fuse, which often blew up in the thrower's own face. A few minutes later some of the lucky enemy who had survived the onslaught, were captured with hands up, rounded up and sent to the rear. They were out of it and would live for another day. Sadly though there were many cases of Germans either putting their hands up to surrender, or showing a white flag, that were put to the bayonet or just shot. Such a thing, and many much worse things do men do when nations fight nations.

It didn't take long for the Germans to range in with small artillery, and the mayhem continued. Now it was their turn to pour in fresh troops for a counter attack. A British captain screamed at a runner: "Tell them we need reinforcements right now!" But the field commanders sent no reinforcements. They had been sent elsewhere, to a more important strategic location. Or maybe the runner never made it back. The captain never knew. His troops would have to either dig in or retreat. They held on for another hour or two, continuing to kill and be killed. In the end, with ammunition low and the men exhausted, they tried a hasty retreat back to their own lines. Many of them, including the captain, were shot in the back.

The same night at division headquarters, a junior officer removed a few coloured pins from a huge map.

The day's action was duly recorded. Result: another couple of thousand men dead, wounded, missing, or captured and not an inch of ground retaken.

Such was Ypres in April 1915.

Oh what a lovely war!

Another nightmare march

Charlie and Wally had lost count of how many night marches they had been on, and nobody had a clue as to where they were going next.

Again not much food, and no time to dry saturated clothes. Poor old Wally, already he was having bad coughing bouts, and a splitting headache that just wouldn't go away. Yet he wasn't as bad as some others, many of the lads of the 12th had hardly any skin left on their feet and ankles, blisters as big as pennies, their socks worn out and the army issue foot powder didn't help. Some were so bad that the medical officer sent them back to the rear in wagons to field hospitals. But not very many. "Lucky bastards" moaned Wally.

The small village lanes around here were congested with troops, wagons, lorries, horses and artillery guns, all going in both directions. Untold thousands of troops and equipment were on the move. Tempers flared when wagons got stuck in the mud holding everything up. It looked like organised chaos.

One officer of the 12th was getting concerned. "It's not right," he said to one of his juniors. "None of our battalion has had any battle experience, just look at them, they look like drowned rats, and none of us has had a good hot decent meal since I don't know when. This is bad planning, very bad planning." He continued getting angrier: "Who in god's name ordered us right here next to the main supply route to the front? The lads can't help noticing the wagons moving south, full of terribly wounded and moaning dying men. I tell you captain, this is very bad for the morale of my raw recruits, and it must be noted in my reports." The captain agreed: "Pardon me sir, but rumour has it that we are to be the reserve in a big push that is coming up soon. Is that correct?" "Can't tell you anything about that, news of that nature is only for the eyes and ears of senior offices. But you will get to know things soon enough. All that I can tell you young man is that none of this fiasco is in the book." The young officer looked puzzled: "How do you mean sir?" Again his senior spoke angrily: "Well it's never been known for raw recruits to be thrown in at the deep end so soon. It takes months to get lads ready for what they have to face, bloody months. So I wouldn't worry too much about rumours of our battalion being in any reserve just yet."

The whole battalion looked a total wreck, even its officers. Anyone looking at them would have thought that they had just done a two-month stint on the front line. They were ragged, wet, hungry, tired and unshaven. Supplies had failed constantly to keep up with them. Now tempers were quick to rise at the least provocation. NCOs were snapped at by the officers, so the NCOs snapped at the privates, who, having no one lower than themselves, snapped back at each other.

Charlie and Wally were trying to scrape the mud off their boots when Wally said: "Charlie, do you think the folk back home in Blighty have any bloody idea what's it like out here?" Charlie grimaced. "Dunno, but I will tell you one thing Wally my mate. There's not so many volunteering to join up now. Not since the papers back home reported about all our dead at Ypres in April. There has been talk and debate in the government, rumour has it that they might have to bring in conscription very soon. I'll tell you one thing though Wally, if I knew beforehand it was going to be like this, I would never in a million years have signed up." It started to rain again.

The night before they had yet again marched from 6.30pm till 3.30am, arriving at another tent city near the village of Ham-En-Artois. There were thousands of tents here for units from all corners of Britain. "Well I guess this is it Wally, this lot here must be the whole 24th Division." They got their mess tins out and joined a queue of about two hundred men. Their reward was a tepid warm stew, two slices of bread with a dollop of jam, plus a large mug of weak looking tea. After downing this five star menu, Charlie walked around trying to cadge a cigarette. Finally succeeding he sat down with Wally and Bill and shared it with them. Bill had been very quiet for a few days, not like him. Although only thirty-one he had aged somewhat in these last few weeks. Indeed all the men had. Now there were no smiles, jokes or laughing. Their whole character had been knocked out of them.

"Roll on demob," moaned Wally.

September 24th 1915

"Right lads, listen up!"

Charlie and the others were gathered together to hear their company commander's address. The officer cleared his throat with a cough:

"Early tomorrow morning, you chaps will hear a thunderous roar of hundreds of artillery guns. It will be deafening, even from this distance. Then on command, thousands of our troops will attack the Germans in the area of Loos. When this attack is successful, and it will be, ourselves, along with the rest of the 24th Division, may be needed to relieve the weary soldiers who have been in the main attack. You will not meet any opposition from the enemy. You will enter the captured German trench system, dig in and hold it until relieved the following day. You've been well prepared for this, and Field Marshal French has every confidence and faith in you. We are going to surprise the Hun lads, push him back, and keep the blaggards running so that they do not have time to dig in again. So good luck, may God be with you, and God save the King. Three cheers for the King!"

"Hip-hip hurray! Hip-hip hurray! Hip-hip hurray!"

"Company… dismissed!" The men trailed off in all directions, a hubbub of noise. Cigarettes were dished out and lit up – at least one supply had caught up with them.

"Well this is it Wally boy, this is definitely fucking it." Charlie, Wally, Bill and a cockney named Archie

Stove made their way to their damp living quarters. "Be a piece of piss tomorrow," said Archie: "lads on the front line have all the hard work to do." He continued: "Looks like we just step in when it's all over, a piece of piss like I just told yer. And another thing," he said: "we might not be called on at all, piece of piss." Private Stove drew on his cigarette and waited for a response from the other three. But no one replied.

The whole battalion cursed when they heard it was to be another night's march towards the front lines. "Every bloody time." moaned Wally. "It's always night marches. Why can't we go in the daytime like civil minded folk?" Charlie shook his head. "How many times have I told you before Wally? We march in the dark so that the enemy doesn't see us. They have spotter planes now. Surprise is a very strong weapon in today's wars. Didn't you listen to any of the lectures we were given back home?" "Nope, just fell asleep at most of em, boring."

At 6.30pm it was once more full pack and on the road again, arriving in the Bethune area at 1.30am. A seven-hour slog in yet more rain. It was pitch black, as they had to hang around for two hours whilst tent accommodation was organised for them. These poor, wet through, and hungry souls were as sick as parrots. A lone voice rang out in the dark night: "Some bastard wants court martialling for this and fucking shot."

September 25th 1915 – Bethune

Dawn finally broke, and all hell let loose. There had been bombardments for days, but this was different. The noise was impossible to describe, a non-stop thunderous roar echoing throughout this flat wasteland. Though about ten miles away the ground trembled as the sky was lit up like a million lightning flashes. Now huge black and grey columns of smoke reached towards the sky. It was like Dante's inferno. Even the officers looked on in awe and amazement. "Some poor bastards are getting it," a voice was heard. "How can anyone live through that lot? Come on Charlie, let's go home." Charlie put his arm around Wally's shoulder. "Like to but maybe after this they might give us a few days back home on leave in good old Blighty."

Sometime later, the barrage ceased as if by magic, now the faint chatter of machine guns could just be heard.

At 10.30am there were more curses as with packs on again they headed towards Vermelles via Beuvry, Sailly and La-Bourse. And they were told that Vermelles was only about three miles from Loos.

September 25th 1915 – Vermelles

A signpost half hidden in the brambles read: "Vermelles – one kilometre". "That's only about half a mile," said Charlie as they trudged on. Dead on noon they were hit by Whizz Bangers. As the German shells started to burst all around them, men scattered like mad to seek cover. Wally and Charlie hid in a bomb crater just behind a low wall. Somehow they had lost sight of Bill. Peeping over, Charlie saw a few men lying about forty feet away. Some lay still, whilst others were wailing and moaning. "Poor bastards, can't we do ote?" It was Wally popping his head over the low wall. "Keep your fucking heads down!" yelled a sergeant, hiding near a barn about ten feet away.

Charlie dragged Wally lower down, their hands tightly holding the tops of their caps as another salvo of shells burst all around them. "These cloth caps are fucking useless Charlie, fucking useless." "Yes, I know. But it's all we got, so do as the sergeant says and keep your head down!" Their ears seemed to burst with the terrible noise, and both Charlie and Wally were trembling with fright. His voice chattering and one arm round Charlie, Wally stuttered: "Charlie, g-g-guess what? I've p-p-pissed myself." A tear fell down his cheek. "Nowt to be ashamed of, I've done the same, but keep yer head down Wally, for Christ's sake keep yer head down."

When it looked like the shelling had ceased, the officers and NCOs rounded up the men and moved wearily through the village of Vermelles. They then headed for the crossroads south west of the small mining community of Le-Rutoire, all the while hearing the sounds of battle raging just ahead of them. They sat huddled at these crossroads all night without any cover until 4am whilst the rest of the 24th Division marched by, heading towards Loos.

This terrible night was spent just walking around talking to various men from other units. From these conversations Charlie learned that lots of men had been killed and wounded by the shells, but luckily none from the 12th Battalion. Many rumours were going around about how the attack had gone, but no-one knew for sure how far the Germans had been pushed back.

None of them could sleep on this terrible night.

September 26th 1915 – Le-Rutoire

Officers arrived with new orders, so up they dragged their weary bodies. None of them had had a wink of sleep all night, and the rain joined in to make it worse. They were all sullen and silent, just putting one tired leg in front of the other. Even the sergeant had stopped his bawling and shouting. He walked with a limp, grimaced his face and hobbled along. Soon they found themselves being herded into a deep, waterlogged trench, twisting and turning ever forward. "Move along A company, move along, there's plenty of room further on, keep moving."

The mist, low cloud and rain persisted on this dark dank day. Charlie's company finally could not go any further as they found themselves squeezed into a sodden firing trench, one side lined with ladders. Every few yards there were mud-caked metal cylinders, connected by copper pipes. A faint, but strangely irritating smell hung in the air. Standing right next to one of the cylinders, Charlie's eyes began to water. He looked up and wished he had not done so. A soldier had died just as he climbed out of the trench, his corpse just visible over the parapet. It was a sickening sight for Charlie and the other raw recruits in his company.

Charlie craned his neck to see where Wally was, finally espying him about twenty yards further up the trench. Squeezing his way through the throng he shouted "Wally, over here!" Wally turned, and his face lit up at seeing his buddy. "Hi Charlie mate, got a spare fag?" After Charlie had lit up two cigarettes, handing one to Wally, he sighed: "This is a right pickle we are in mate, and make no mistake about that." "Yeah but we will look after each other won't we mate?" replied Wally. "Sure we will, sure we will Wally."

"Right, now listen up everybody. Shut up you lot down there!" All eyes turned to a young officer further down the trench. "We are now holding the first line of the English trenches. It was from here that our brave boys attacked the German lines yesterday. And we have heard they were most successful. The major has just returned from HQ and was informed that all is going to plan. The enemy is disrupted and on the run in some places". A loud cheering and whistling went up at this point. "When you get out of this trench, you can just make out Tower Bridge, the double pithead at

Loos to your right. In front of you is what's left of the small mining village of Hulluch. We will advance past it toward the next village, Vendin-Le-Viel. We will be well behind the 72nd and 71st Brigades and whatever is left of the Hun, they will deal with." There were mumbles of

relief at this last bit of news. And some even gave a twisted smile.

Lecture over, the officer checked his watch, nodded to a sergeant, then blew his whistle. The sergeant climbed out of the trench and beckoned the men forwards. Clambering out they all walked east, some even lighting up their cigarettes. Before them lay flat, open ground. Every house, cottage and dwelling was just a pile of rubble. Mud-filled bomb craters in their hundreds covered this desolate place.

The cracks of rifles and the sounds of machine gun fire grew louder to their right, though it sounded a good way off. A few yards along more bodies and parts of bodies lay in their path. Charlie and the others stopped and hesitated. "Keep moving, keep moving," a sergeant yelled. "You can't help em now, so keep moving!" Charlie felt absolutely sick and threw up. He was no longer wet, hungry, nor was he tired! No. He was absolutely saturated, starving to death, and completely exhausted.

The battalion crept forward slowly, now the sounds of zzip-zzip rang out. Wally crumbled down with a bullet in the knee, shredding his cartilage to bits. Although he yelled out in agony, his only thought as he lay in pain was: "Well this will get me my one way ticket back to Blighty out of this hell hole." He saw Charlie about thirty yards ahead, advancing ever onwards. "Charlie, Charlie!"

At the sounds of the sniper fire and Wally's screams most of the men froze, some looked for some kind of protection. But there was none. Some knelt down. "Get up, get up, keep moving, damn you! Move, I say move!"

Charlie had heard that the British army shoots cowards. So he did as ordered, though he was petrified.

Screaming high explosive howitzer shells passed high over the shaking men's heads, and a sense of relief came to them all as they realised that they were hitting targets further back.

Charlie staggered on and saw more men going down. Stretcher bearers were running here and there. Further back Wally caught sight of two of them heading towards him. "Over here, over here!" He tried to shout as loud as he could, but the sound of battle swallowed up his cries for help. The stretcher bearers altered direction and headed towards another unfortunate casualty elsewhere. Wally's pain grew more intense and he drifted into unconsciousness and knew no more.

The acrid stench of cordite and the few pockets of gas that still hung around made many halt, stutter and throw up. Yet there was no let-up for these men. "Move, move I say, damn you move, advance, advance!" The nightmare of ever increasing chaos and bedlam continued, and these men advanced for the glory of Great Britain, the glorious Empire, the King and God almighty.

Charlie

Charlie was by now at about his wits end. A lonely soul, a lost man in this godforsaken hellhole that was Northern France, September the 26th 1915. He knew that soon he could not put another step forwards. He was spent.

The German sniper glanced with his eagle eyes, squinted and thought: "Ah, yah." This time just one zzip! A man dropped like a lead weight to the ground, a neat red hole in the side of his temple. The sergeant would never give out any more orders. A few yards away Charlie thought it couldn't get any worse, when all of a sudden shells started to explode around them. He heard the terrible screams of men behind him. "I wonder where Wally's got to?" he thought.

Black smoke from these enemy shells was now swirling all around the area. Charlie entered this fog like a man passing through the black gates of hell.

A German six-inch high explosive artillery shell whined its way up into the sky, reached its highest trajectory point, and then screeched down towards the earth in its death dive. It thudded into the ground just five feet in front of Charlie. It detonated instantly, and Charlie was blown up and scattered into a million pieces.

End

Charlie's Battle

By People's Histreh

The Battle of Loos was fought in the early autumn of 1915 in a mining area in northern France, not far from the Belgian border.

Its first day, the 25th September, saw the largest land battle ever fought by British troops up to that point in time. Although soon to be dwarfed by the campaigns yet to come, the Battle of Loos is often mentioned in histories of the war, marking the first time British troops used chemical weapons in combat and the first attack involving large numbers of New Army troops.[1]

The Battle of Loos had been doomed from its very conception, its outcome worsened by failures in the subsequent planning and preparations, as well as poor decision-making during the attack. It resulted in tens of thousands of casualties on both sides, without the attackers being able to achieve any discernible military success. The offensive is however noteworthy for that

---

1 Also known as Kitchener's Armies, these consisted of the volunteers who had signed up after the war broke out in August 1914. Before the Battle at Loos, New Army units had already been deployed in different theatres of war. In early August 1915 New Army troops, including the 9th Battalion Sherwood Foresters, took part in the Sulva Bay landings at Gallipoli. Remaining true to the callous overconfidence that forms the bedrock of so much military planning, the 9th Foresters and the rest of the 11th Division, inexperienced troops recruited from some of the most land-locked areas in Britain, were ordered to attempt an ambitious amphibious landing, equipped with and supported by nothing more than the kit they could carry in the knapsacks. Guess what happened.

very reason, as British military commanders had not, at least in the beginning, aimed at a military victory as the key outcome of this battle.

This chapter contextualises Colin's fictionalised story of Charlie Brett's experiences in France. Although finding himself in the thick of things, it can be assumed that the real Charlie had also been kept largely ignorant of the events which would result in his death on the 26th September, the second day of the battle.

The wider context

By the summer of 1915, the stalemate on the Western Front had long – and in many places literally – been cemented.

When war broke out the previous year, the German military aimed for a quick and decisive victory against the French Army, which was expected to be assisted only by a tokenistic British Expeditionary Force (BEF). To knock out their main opponent in the West would have enabled the German Empire to throw all its might against the slowly mobilising colossus that was Tsarist Russia.

This plan failed (numerous libraries have been filled debating the reasons), for instance due to the Belgian army slowing down the German troops and the British force turning out to be not quite as tokenistic as expected. The French Army finally managed to hold and turn the German advance in early September 1914.

In those first weeks both sides suffered previously unparalleled casualties, but neither was decisively defeated. Unsuccessful flanking manoeuvres and further fierce fighting quickly turned into a stalemate.

By the onset of winter, millions of soldiers on the Western Front were living in a rudimentary version of what remains the most defining feature of World War One, a system of trenches and fortified strongpoints stretching for hundreds of miles through Belgium and France.

On the Eastern Front German troops had repulsed the initial attacks by Russian Armies. Although the Tsarist troops took horrendous casualties, they had more success in fighting the Austro-Hungarians, one of the key German allies. Able to tap into vast reserves, especially of human lives, the Tsar's regime would throw its soldiers time and again against the German Armies. Although the war on the Eastern Front would play out rather differently than in the West, those initial encounters also resulted in neither side having been able to decisively defeat the other, setting the scene for further clashes to come.

Still thinking that the stalemate in the West could only be a temporary state of affairs, it dawned only very slowly on most commanders that neither side would destroy their opponent by continuing to order their troops to link arms, shout hooray and rush forwards. This did not however stop all sides from experimenting with more unusual ways of killing and maiming people.

Many of these 'new' weapons and tactics were actually rather ancient ones, most notably mining. Tunnelling underneath each other's defences, trying to blow them up from below soon became a common and particularly nasty way to fight and die in the war. Some weapons were however genuinely new, the ascent of chemical warfare possibly being the most (in-)famous example. Various armies had dabbled with this technology during the earliest stages of the war, but poison gas made its first notable appearance on the Western Front during the German attacks on the Belgium city of Ypres in spring 1915.[2]

Throughout 1915 the German Armies' efforts were primarily focussed on the Eastern Front, whilst in the West the French Armies took the lead in trying to break the stalemate. A number of offensives resulted in very little other than adding another few hundred thousand names to the ever growing casualty lists, before the attacks ran out of steam and both sides resumed 'normal' trench warfare, i.e. hostilities on a relatively constant, but comparably low level.[3]

An Anglo-French attempt to sidestep the stalemate in the West by attacking the Ottoman Empire, the German's most important ally, at Gallipoli quickly proved to be a grandiose, half-baked and ill-executed

---

2 The introduction of poison gas to the battlefields set a pattern which would be repeated in regard to various other 'innovations'. When it was first used at Ypres, it was surprisingly successful (i.e. it killed, wounded and terrified lots of people), but that 'success' also came as a surprise to the German troops, who were not prepared to fully exploit their brief opportunity. By the time the weapon was used again, the element of surprise had largely been lost, the other side begun to come up with rudimentary countermeasures and would before long use the weapon themselves. When looking at these new technologies, it should not be forgotten that some of the most influential pieces of equipment were technically not even weapons, most notably barbed wire, which would come to dominate the battlefields.

3 See SHE; p103: "The story of the Western Front in 1915 is essentially one of repeated attempts to achieve a breakthrough that failed and degenerated into attrition." True words, however that also seems to be very much the case in 1916 and 1917. There is a lot to be said about trench warfare, attrition and how troops kept developing rather sophisticated ways of combat avoidance during periods of stagnant trench warfare, something often referred to as a system of live-and-let-live.

idea, driven by a callous overestimation of the Allies' capabilities and a blatantly racist underestimation of the Ottoman Armies.

Although the British Army did mount attacks on the Western Front in 1915, they did so in support of much grander French offensives, and remained at this stage only a junior partner in the war.

The French and German conscript armies were millions strong when they went to war in 1914. Although made up of professional soldiers, the British Army was tiny in comparison, having been designed to uphold and expand British rule in colonies all over the globe,[4] not to fight mass armies in Europe. By mid-1915 the ranks of that original Regular Army had been utterly depleted.

Although masses of fresh volunteers had signed up to the New Armies, they were still being trained back in Britain, and in many areas the lines were held by a mix of older reservists and the weekend soldiers of the Territorial Army. Although sufficient to keep the German Armies at bay, and starting to be significantly reinforced,[5] British troops were neither numerous enough nor was wartime production yet able to turn out the equipment which would be needed to mount the kind of offensives seen from 1916 onwards.

---

4 The spirit of the British Army during much of the latter half of the nineteenth century might be best caught by this: BEL; p41: "Whatever happens, we have got, the Maxim Gun, and they have not."

5 The BEF had nominally grown by almost 60 percent between May and August 1915, but still only amounted to about twenty percent of all allied divisions on the Western Front.

Despite the continued stalemate on the Western Front, the tide of war seemed to have turned against the Allies during the summer of 1915. There had been a series of disasters for the Russian troops on the Eastern Front. Although Italy had joined the war on the allied side, they had not been able to make any significant advances against the Austro-Hungarian Empire. Furthermore Bulgaria had joined the war on the side of the Germans, increasing the pressure on Serbia, the minor allied power whose conflicts with the Austro-Hungarians had been the trigger for this whole wretched affair.

This formed the background to mounting political pressure to keep the German Armies occupied on the Western Front to indirectly support the Tsarist Armies in the east. The French government was not prepared to mount further attacks if the British Army would continue a defensive stance, waiting to be further reinforced by the millions of volunteers and for their naval blockade to starve out the German Empire.

Therefore concerns about the state of the alliance were very real amongst British military and political elites and calls grew louder for a renewed offensive on the Western Front, fought with the full commitment of the British Army.[6]

---

6 As always, there are many other aspects to that story, not least complex politics within the British Army itself, with the commanders of the BEF having concerns that they needed to use their growing strength in order to stop more equipment and troops being redirected to other theatres of war.

Plans and preparations

The basic idea for a new Anglo-French offensive on the Western Front in late 1915 was for British troops to support yet another grand French offensive by launching a simultaneous attack near Loos, hoping to force the German Armies to redirect some of their reserves to defend their lines, diverting them from the area of the main French advance.

The ground chosen by the French for the British attack very much favoured the German defenders. They controlled the high ground and their lines had been heavily fortified, for instance with many machine gun positions concealed in the cellars of ruined pit villages. Any attacker would have to cross over flat, open ground, offering easy targets for German rifle and machine gun fire, whilst the defenders' artillery could effectively be directed from the many observation posts on top of slack heaps.

Neither John French, at the time the commander in chief of all British forces on the Western Front, nor the notorious Douglas Haig, then in command of the British 1st Army, which was due to deliver the attack,[7] were all too keen on the coming offensive. For once neither seemed to indulge in any fantasies of achieving

---

[7] By summer 1915 it was no longer a question whether or not John French was in way over his head as commander of the BEF. It was merely unknown when he would lose his command. Haig was one of many who had been busy undermining the rather incompetent commander in chief and his personal dislike for French is well documented. See e.g. SHE/BOU; p151: Just before the Battle of Loos Haig described French as looking: "a little better, but older and fatter."

a decisive breakthrough which would sweep the Huns all the way back to Berlin by Christmas. They were however persuaded to commit to an attack at Loos, undertaken with "the maximum force […] available". (SHE/BOU; p136) Both men were fully aware what this would mean. During lunch at his chateau on the 17th August, French ordered Haig to "attack on as wide a front as possible", knowing that "we must have big losses […] to achieve any result." (ibid.) Two days later, Haig was visited by the Minister for War, Horatio Kitchener, Haig noting in his diaries:

> "After washing his hands Lord Kitchener came into my writing room upstairs saying he had been anxious to […] talk with me. The Russians, he said, had been severely handled and it was doubtful how much longer their Armies would withstand the German blows. Up to the present he had favoured a policy of an active defence in France until such time as all our forces were ready to strike. The situation which had arisen in Russia had caused him to modify these views. He now felt that the Allies must act vigorously in order to take some of the pressure off Russia if possible. He had heard […] that Sir J[ohn] French did not mean to co-operate to the utmost of his power when the French attacked in September. [Kitchener] had noticed that the French were anxiously watching the British on their left[8] and he

---

8 'Up the line', 'down the line', 'on our left', 'on our right', all these directions can be a bit confusing. They were always given from the point of view of an imaginary observer looking from the British and French lines towards the German trenches. 'Up the line', or going 'left' meant going along the twisting and turning front lines towards the North Sea, 'down the line', or 'right' meant moving towards Switzerland.

> had decided that we 'must act with all our energy, and do our utmost to help the French, even though by doing so we suffer very heavy losses indeed.'" (SHE/BOU; p137)

So the stage was set for the tragedy to come. The British would attack to support the Russian and French Armies, even though they were not ready for it and an attack at Loos would surely result in very heavy losses. Haig bowed to the pressure at least partly due to concerns for his own career,[9] but once he committed to the idea, Haig devoted himself to an all-out attack in the Loos sector. He knew that if the attack would turn out to be a 'success', he would be a hero and if not, his concerns were on record and he might even be able to use this to further undermine John French's position.

The British troops ordered to climb out of their trenches would find themselves not only going up against well-prepared positions after crossing extremely unfavourable terrain, they would also have to do so without much supporting fire from their artillery. Both the number of guns and the stocks of ammunition available were very much restricted. The final plans set out four separate twelve hour barrages over four consecutive days. Albeit terrifying and sure to kill and maim many individual German soldiers, this

---

9 See HAR; p158: "[Haig] was too ambitious and too canny to try to resist simultaneous pressure from Joffre, [John French] and the British government, as represented by Kitchener. In the climate of August-September 1915 he felt he had no choice but to mount a major offensive in the Loos sector."

would not only be insufficient to destroy their defences, but also give the defenders the opportunity to repair any damage done, especially to the barbed wire entanglements in front of their trenches.[10]

British planners knew this and put much hope on the use of poison gas (see e.g. WO95/158/1; p7). It was hoped that chlorine gas could kill, incapacitate or rout many defenders, allowing the British infantry to take their trenches without too much opposition. Poison gas cylinders were installed in the British front line trenches and connected through a system of pipes. As the valves were opened, the gas, heavier than air, would build up in a big cloud which, it was hoped, would float towards the German trenches if the wind was blowing in the right direction at the right strength.

Having taken the decision to attack on a wide front with pretty much all available forces, British planners

---

[10] Despite widely held perceptions about the dominance of the machine gun during World War One, the biggest killer was artillery fire, accounting for about sixty percent of all casualties amongst the British troops. Artillery was crucial on the defence and the attack, used during the former to shatter advancing waves of troops and on the attack to destroy defenders' trenches and smash gaps through their wire entanglements. Whereas in the earlier, and – by World War One standards – 'successful', battle of Neuve Chapelle, there had been one gun for every six yards of the frontline to be attacked, at Loos there was one gun for every 141 yards. Later battles would prove that overwhelming firepower was not enough to win battles, but they could be lost even faster without it. For all the critique of a lack of troops, guns and ammunition available at Loos, a look down the line at the French Army's offensive makes one thing clear: there was no way of 'winning' these battles. The French troops would attack in far greater numbers and with ample artillery support, but also failed to force any decisive outcome, whilst suffering terrible losses.

also faced a problem regarding the all-important issue of reserves. Previous battles had demonstrated that it was possible to take a few trenches and thus push their opponents some dozen or a few hundred yards back, provided the attackers were willing to do so at the price of countless lives. It was however much more difficult to hold such 'gains', let alone push them any further, given that the attacking units would not only be depleted, but also exhausted following the enormous physical and psychological strains during their initial advance. Therefore it had proven crucial to have fresh troops available behind the line to support the initial waves of attackers.

Given the commitment of so many troops to the initial attacks, there was only one body of troops available to be that reserve, the XI Corps, incorporating Charlie Brett's 12th Battalion Sherwood Foresters. Almost everyone in the two divisions of the XI Corps which had been assigned as reserves for the attack were inexperienced soldiers whose training had been patchy at best. To further complicate matters, they were not under Haig's command, but would have to be 'released' by John French before Haig could issue any orders to them, something French proved reluctant to do until the very last minute.[11]

---

11 Much of the debates in the aftermath of the failed battle, especially Haig's very successful attempt to firmly pin the blame on French, would revolve around this issue, some details of which remain debated to this day, partially due to the extensive and complex political manoeuvers after the battle.

As implied in Colin's story and exemplified by various passages in the 12th Foresters *War Diary* (see appendices), Charlie and his mates were not at all prepared to play a potentially crucial role in a major offensive. Their battalion had only been formed on the 1st October 1914. In April 1915 they had been designated as a pioneer battalion,[12] i.e. a unit of: "fighting infantry but with specific skills in road making, entrenching and demolition." (STA/LEE; p83) As so many other units in the New Armies, they underwent months of (more or less intense) training whilst still lacking much of their equipment. It is not entirely clear when the 12th Foresters were issued with uniforms, weapons, and all the other bits of army kit, but it seems that it was not until they were moved to Aldershot in August 1915 that they were even given "a change of clothes and some protection against the almost continuous rain." (HOU/LEI; p6)

It was only in late August 1915, about one month before they were expected to take part in their first battle, that the 12th Foresters had any weapons drill at all, and they only got another chance to get a little bit more experience with rifles, machine guns and grenades after they arrived in France.

---

[12] In an effort to very much simplify a bafflingly complex, inconsistent and constantly changing structure, we can state here that the British Army in World War One incorporated units of unarmed labourers as well as combat troops, although the latter were at all times also ordered to carry out countless chores, for instance digging trenches or hauling supplies. Being part of the fighting infantry, pioneer battalions could well find themselves in combat roles, but their primary function was to act as specialised labourers in and behind the lines.

Despite their lack of experience and training, Charlie and his mates left the village of Saint-Denœux on the afternoon of the 21st September, marching towards the front lines to reinforce the 75,000 troops Haig would commit to the attack at Loos.

In the run up to the battle Haig's confidence appears to have grown and he seems to have convinced himself that the battle was not merely a symbolic demonstration of Britain's commitment to the war effort, but that he could actually turn this into a significant military victory, if only the wind would be favourable to launch the gas attack. He was not the only British officer who shared that confidence.

As it turned out they were wrong.

Loos – Day One

On September 25th the wind, crucial in the British plan that depended so much on the 'successful' deployment of poison gas, did not appear favourable. For a while Haig wavered whether he should even give the order to release it, but at "5.15[am] I said 'Carry on'." (SHE/BOU; p153)

So began what Haig described as the "greatest battle in the world's history" (ibid). The guns ceased firing and the valves on the gas cylinders were opened. Immediately things began to go wrong. Whereas in some areas the chlorine duly started to drift towards the German lines, elsewhere the poison clouds were blown right back into the massed British ranks, injuring and killing soldiers and creating chaos and confusion before the troops had even left their trenches.

Shortly afterwards tens of thousands of British soldiers clambered out of their lines. A lot of them walked straight into a withering fire from the German defenders. Whereas the gas had worked in some places, many German troops had been affected little or not at all, whilst the British advance was severely obstructed by all the wire entanglements which had been left undamaged by the bombardment. Some units were shot to pieces as soon as they went over the top, a few got lucky and managed to take part of the German line suffering 'only' ten or fifteen percent casualties. Others managed to conquer a position or overrun a hilltop, but in doing so took such extreme losses that the survivors had to fall back or would be pushed back by the inevitable German counter attacks – which were often just as suicidal as the initial advances by the British. In the horrifying chaos of battle, shells fell indiscriminately and soldiers found themselves under fire from areas they believed to be under the control of their own side.

Reading accounts of this and many other battles, it seems not surprising that thousands were killed or maimed within minutes. What is much more puzzling is the fact that there were some 'successes' at all. At the end of that day, British troops did overrun the town of Loos itself, as well as some of their other targets. Their massed ranks had managed to break into and take control of the first line of German defences and in a few places briefly made incursions into the defenders' second line. But whatever hopes Haig may have held after a few weeks of self-delusion, this attack had not been a decisive blow. Once more a break-through the German lines had not been achieved, it had merely been shown again that a break-in was possible, as long as the attackers were willing to pay for it with extreme casualties.

Harris' "conservative" estimate of British casualties on that first day of the Battle of Loos are as high as 470 officers and 15,000 other ranks killed, wounded or missing (HAR; p173).[13]

---

[13] Apparently this meant that in relation to the numbers of troops involved, losses had been even worse than they would be on the notorious first day of fighting at the Somme on the 1st July 1916.

Behind the lines, Haig had very little control over events on the ground once he had given the order to press ahead.[14] The reports that did eventually get through to him apparently painted a very optimistic picture of what was happening. Halfway through the day, Haig believed that there was a fleeting opportunity to break through the German lines. After French eventually granted Haig's request to release the reserves, Haig ordered them at 2.30pm to push into what he thought to be a gap in the German defences.

But not only was there no gap, at this point Charlie, the 12th Foresters, and most of the other reserves were still miles behind the lines, exhausted by their often diverted march through torrential rain.[15]

---

[14] It has been argued that World War One "stands as the only period in history in which high commanders were mute" (SHE; p99), that they could often do little but to decide when to commit the reserves, which would more often than not arrive late and in the (by then) wrong location. In earlier periods battles had been fought on a much smaller scale, whereas later technological advances, especially radios, would give commanders more of an idea what was actually happening and enable them to give their orders. Therefore before and after the era commanders were usually able to exert some degree of control, although it is a different matter whether or not that control was in any way sensible. During World War One the most common way to get reports back and orders forth was to send runners, given that telephone wires were vulnerable to shellfire and wireless technology was still in its infancy. For obvious reasons this was not too efficient for the commanders and very dangerous for those doing the running. For the units who might receive orders hours after they were given these instructions often turned out to be nonsensical or worse.

[15] Losing out on this imagined opportunity because the reserves had not been available to go into action on the 25th became one of Haig's core criticisms of French during the dealing and scheming which followed the battle.

Loos – Day Two

By the early hours of the 26th September, the Germans had had plenty of time to reinforce their largely undamaged second line of defences. The British lines remained improvised, disorganised and in one place featured a gap of almost 1,500 yards.[16] Many units which had attacked the previous day had taken severe casualties and all of them were exhausted. By now the reserves had finally reached the front lines, but were worn-out themselves.

Charlie's unit had been on the march for the last five days, mostly moving at night, often in very bad weather.[17] We do not know exactly how well the 12th Foresters had been supplied during that time, but there are a number of reports that the reserve troops at Loos had not got much food on their way to the

---

16 During the war attackers not only had to overcome well-entrenched opposition, in doing so they also made it much harder to consolidate their new positions. The ground taken had been disrupted by shells, and still featured wire entanglements and other obstacles. There would not yet be any communication trenches linking the newly taken foremost positions to the roads and railheads behind the lines, meaning that supplies and people had to cross the former no-man's-land in order to shore up the new front line trenches. At the same time the defenders, who would usually fall back to prepared positions, could rely on most of their logistics remaining intact.

17 It is hard to estimate correctly the distance marched by Charlie and his comrades based on (modern and contemporary) maps. It must also be assumed that especially the last leg of their march towards the battle, from Bethune to Le Rutoire, was anything but straightforward, with the battalion being repeatedly diverted in the semi-organised chaos of troops and supplies behind the lines. It seems sure that almost all the marching by Charlie and his mates was done by night, most of it in three night marches on the 21st, 22nd and 24th September.

battle, let alone having had any chance to get some hot food and proper rest.

Haig was apparently still optimistic of being able to turn this battle into a significant victory, and was about to throw Charlie and his mates against the German second line. But whereas the attackers on the previous day had some familiarity with the terrain, at least some artillery support, and their advance had partly been obscured by clouds of smoke and gas, Charlie and his comrades were pretty much on their own.

When the order to attack came, the reserves, often along with troops who had already been engaged the previous day, advanced and were in most areas quickly shot to pieces. All in all the two reserve divisions lost well over 8,000 troops in the course of that day.[18] Harris described how:

> "[…] large sections fell back in a state of disorder that, at least in some instances, amounted to rout. […] The 24th Division and the 21st Division were in such a state of shock and demoralisation by the night of 26 September that it was imperative to take them off the battlefield without delay." (HAR; pp175-6)

It seems that the only reason why Charlie's battalion 'only' suffered losses of about ten percent was that they ended up being the reserves' reserves. As such they had advanced behind other units from 11am

[18] At full textbook strength, a World War One British division was made up of around 10-12,000 troops. Even if it is assumed that these two divisions were at full strength, the figures mean that about one in three soldiers became a casualty.

as part of the general attack. All in all they had got as far as a mile from their starting point, advancing a few hundred yards beyond the former British firing trenches to the road between Loos and Hulluch. The troops ahead and to the side of the 12th Foresters came under heavy cross-fire and were forced to retire, leaving them alone in the front lines. There they remained for about an hour and a half, waiting in vain for any orders before retreating themselves, falling back to what had been the German first line. At 2am that night they were relieved by other troops and marched out of the front lines. The initial count listed five soldiers to have been killed outright, 62 others wounded and another 29 missing.[19]

When and how Charlie Brett died during the 12th Foresters' brief and pointless advance remains unknown. Hopefully his end was as instantaneous as in Colin's story.

---

[19] Assuming the 12th Foresters were at textbook strength, the total of 96 casualties amounted to losses of pretty much ten percent. According to the COMMONWEALTH GRAVES DATABASE, nine soldiers from the 12th Foresters died on the 26th September, another one died from his wounds a couple of days later. See also the casualty list in the appendices.

Aftermath

As with so many World War One battles, it is not that easy to pinpoint exactly when the Battle of Loos ended. A final British assault failed on the 13th October, marking the official end of the battle. The actual offensive had however almost immediately run out of steam and turned into a number of fierce, more localised engagements, with both sides wrestling for control of one strongpoint or another. Within a couple of months, the lines had stabilised again, after some of the ground taken by the British on the 25th September had been lost. Trench warfare resumed along slightly shifted lines. Soldiers continued to be killed and wounded, but they were no longer battle casualties, but what was often referred to as 'trench wastage'.

In terms of making and sustaining any significant advance, let alone breaking through the German lines, Loos had been a failure.

British casualties had been terrible. Although new records would be set before long, losses amounted to an incomprehensible 50,000 persons, of which around 6,000 had been killed and another 16,000 missing, many of whom would have died as well. The Germans, far from being shy in sending wave after wave to their deaths trying to retake some of their lost positions, suffered about half of the British casualties.

Therefore also in terms of attrition, a concept which would very soon begin to dominate the minds of strategists on all sides, Loos had been a failure.

Thinking back to the start of this whole tragedy, a 'victory' as such had never been the primary object. Plans for this offensive had started with the perceived need to reassure the other allies that Britain was fully committed to the war effort and would not sit by as the other major powers suffered blow after blow. Initially, the military objectives had been focussed on distracting the German war machine, supporting the other allied forces in general, and the latest (unsuccessful) attempt at a 'Big Push' by the French Army in particular. The fact that the British attack failed so decisively is a strong indicator that the British Army in the autumn of 1915 did not (yet) have the strength to significantly distract the German colossus, let alone defeat it. And whatever some senior British officers may have fantasised in the immediate run-up to the attack, Haig's diary entries in the early planning stages make it very clear that it was well known that the offensive would fail.[20]

Indeed, the primary aim of the Battle of Loos appears to have been making a grand gesture,

---

20 See SHE/BOU; pp128-9: Before Haig had committed to the attack, he had noted in his diary: "Tuesday 22 June – [The] Enemy has greatly strengthened his position. A second line with wire entanglement is distinctly visible. [After explaining that limited gains could be made he continues:] it would not be possible to advance beyond, because our own artillery could not support us […]. On the other hand the Enemy has excellent observing stations for his artillery [and his] defences are now so strong that they can only be taken by siege methods […] the ground above is so swept by gun and machine gun and rifle fire that an advance in the open, except by night, is impossible." An Anglo-French conference in June 1915 had confirmed the widely held view that the British Army was in no shape for a major offensive.

demonstrating beyond all doubt Britain's commitment to its allies and the war effort, whether or not the British Army was actually able to do anything but hold their part of the line.

British military and civilian elites correctly assumed that taking "very heavy losses indeed" on this occasion would not make much difference to British fighting power in the long run. The majority of the volunteers had not yet arrived in France, and war production was steadily gathering pace. Therefore, sacrificing part of the first batch of volunteers and some of the remnants of the Regular and Territorial Forces would not result in Britain losing the war, especially whilst the Germans were focussing their efforts elsewhere. So to those who bought into the sick and twisted logic of this war, the Battle of Loos made sense as losing some ten thousand soldiers to shore up the alliance seemed a logical thing to do.

It was Charlie and the many other victims of the battle on both sides who paid the price. What drove that price even higher seems to have been that Haig and various others convinced themselves that they could actually turn this battle into a significant military victory. Harris argues that Haig maintained this belief on the morning of the 26th September, giving orders to renew the attacks of the previous day:

> "Haig could not get it out of his head that he was on the cusp of a tremendous victory. He continued to give orders based on this erroneous reading of the battle. Thus the bloody gesture of alliance solidarity on which Kitchener had insisted

> became, under Haig's direction, much bloodier and more self-destructive than was really necessary." (HAR; p177)

Harris' lines are a good example for a fundamental issue that unites the Donkey-bashing Clark, the new revisionist Sheffield, the much more moderate Harris and so many other authors. Whether they defend or criticise how the war was fought, they only ever debate the conduct of the war, not the war itself. They ignore the political and economic system that had made this conflict possible, and are simply critical (to very different degrees) of all the stupid decisions which cost so many more lives than may have been "necessary".

Colin states that his grandfather was murdered by his officers. That is entirely correct. It was obvious that his unit's advance would fail. It had been obvious that the whole attack on Loos was doomed from its conception. But looking into the reasons why Charlie and all the others were told to attack anyway exemplifies not only that organised mass murder is at the very core of what any army is about, but that once someone buys into the twisted logic of power politics involving military forces, mass murder quickly becomes a regrettable necessity.

For us, merely criticising Haig for giving stupid orders or reaffirming the well-known fact that John French was utterly incompetent, and that "lessons" had not been learned from previous disasters really misses the point. We see the problem in *the fact that there was a war in the first place.* We want to focus our anger at the state of the societies who engaged in this conflict, whose political and socio-economical organisation not only enabled the war, but also stopped a sufficient number of people on all sides from seeing reason. Charlie and all the others found themselves in a situation where advancing into shell and machine gun fire seemed saner and more logical than deserting en masse and going home – ideally after using their guns against those who sent them into this war. This may become understandable as we try to reconstruct some of these individuals' experiences, but that does not make it any less tragic.[21]

As to the aftermath of the battle for the survivors of Charlie's battalion: following their first experience of battle, the 12th Foresters' spent a few days behind the lines. They were congratulated for their actions on the 26th September, and did quite a bit of "salvage" work and burying the dead. They spent the remainder of the war on the Western Front, being sent up and down the line, digging many more trenches, many more graves and taking part in further battles. By the 11th November 1918, 224 persons had died whilst serving with the battalion. The 12th Foresters remain very notable as some of them started the incredible satirical trench newspaper known as the *Wipers Times*, thus leaving an extraordinary and hilarious legacy.

The extent of British losses at Loos and just how little there was to show for them did cause quite a stir. Haig managed to play his cards very cleverly, even

21 Indeed, much of our work around death sentences and mutinies in the British Army is closely connected to the question why soldiers obeyed.

though his decisions played a rather crucial part in this attack being a debacle on such a scale. Indeed, Haig quickly showed just how astute a political beast he could be. French however had already proved beyond doubt that he was quite inept at managing the BEF. The shambles of the Loos Battle, especially the issues regarding the release of the reserves, turned out to be the final nail in the coffin of his career. By the end of the year Haig replaced French as commander in chief of all British Empire troops on the Western Front.[22]

As to the victims of Loos on both sides of no-man's land: whether or not they had been physically present at the battle and whether or not they survived the slaughter and its aftermath, what would become little more than an extensive footnote in most histories of the war would often overshadow the rest of their lives. Many of those who came out of the fighting physically unharmed would continue to be haunted by it.[23] Those injured and maimed in combat would forever bear their visible and invisible scars. And as always in war, the number of those affected was far greater than just the people who had actually taken

22 The fact that the historiography of the battle has made so much of this issue may be partly down to Haig playing that card so successfully against French.

23 A very vivid impression of this can be gained by watching one of the *Great War Interviews* available on the BBC IPLAYER. Edward Glendinning, from a different battalion of the Sherwood Foresters, also took part in the Battle of Loos. When he was interviewed in 1963, he still could hear the screams of wounded comrades pleading for water.

part in the fighting, but included all their families and friends.

We do not know when Charlie's folks got word of his death. It is possible that they initially thought that he had only been wounded, which possibly even raised hopes of him returning home soon.[24] There could however have been no doubt by the following April, when the War Office granted "the widow of No. 20652 Pte Charles Brett […] a Pension of 21 [shilling] a week, for herself and two children […]." In November 1916 the family received what appears to have been Charlie's outstanding army pay, a sum of two pound, five shillings and four pence. The paper trail left by Charlie in the army records ends in July 1919 with a note stating that his widow received a three pound "War Gratuity". He has no known grave.

Charlie's family would suffer further devastating losses during the war and its immediate aftermath: in 1918 two of Charlie's sons were killed in France. The younger son Jack died on the 15th June, William on the 9th October. Having been born in 1898 and 1899, neither lived to see their twenty-first birthday. Charlie's younger brother Henry, born around 1880, who had

---

24 The only reference to Charlie in a local newspaper is in a casualty report printed in *The Derby Daily Telegraph* on Friday, 22nd October 1915, listing: "Pte. C. Brett (20652)" among the names of wounded soldiers. It is unknown if the family ever saw the paper and whether this would have been the first they heard of Charlie, or if they had already got word of him having been killed. It seems that this report was however an error rather than an indication that Charlie died of wounds after the battle as all other records, such as his service record, list him as having been killed on the 26th September.

been a driver in an artillery unit, died on the 12th December 1918 in a military hospital in Nottingham. He had contracted pneumonia and died after six days, quite possibly having previously contracted the so-called Spanish Flu.[25]

Roughly a quarter of a century after Charlie' death, Charlie's youngest son Albert became the father of a (back then presumably hatless and non-smoking) tiny Colin.

Even before our comrade was born, his life had already been touched by war, which had forever changed the story of his whole family by taking away his grandad, two uncles and a great-uncle.

Before long Colin's life would be affected by another global war.

---

[25] Jack Brett's soldier number was 144834, William's 55871 and Henry's 771120. Jack and William are buried in France, Henry in Nottingham's General Cemetery. The spread of the Spanish Flu, one of the deadliest pandemics in human history is estimated to have led to between 50 and 100 million deaths between 1918 and 1920. Many victims apparently died from bacterial pneumonia following an infection with the influenza virus. The global spread of the disease was greatly assisted by the war and its aftermath, with millions living in cramped conditions, being moved around the world in troop ships, etc.

Appendices

Reading list

There are countless books on all aspects of World War One. Many are excellent, many others utter rubbish.

This reading list can only ever be a signpost for the interested reader.

We included quotes from and directly referred to the following books:

BEAVER, PATRICK/ET AL (eds.; 2014 – originally published 1916-1918): *The Wipers Times – The Complete Series of the Famous Wartime Trench Newspaper*; Max Press; London.

How do many people deal with extreme situations? They make jokes. This brilliant edition of the satirical newspaper written, produced and distributed on the Western Front provides fascinating insights into the everyday lives of soldiers and how they perceived what they went through. It is also absolutely hilarious.

BELLOC, JOSEPH HPR (1898): *The Modern Traveller*; Edward Arnold; London. Referenced as: BEL.

CLARK, ALAN (1961): *The Donkeys*; Pimlico; London.

For all its problems, this remains a classic.

HARRIS, JP (2008): *Douglas Haig and the First World War*; Cambridge University Press; Cambridge. Referenced as: HAR.

A good book about Haig. Acknowledges the work of the new revisionists and paints a more nuanced picture, but does not shy away from Haig-bashing either. Contains a well-referenced chapter on the Battle of Loos.

HOBSBAWM, ERIC: *The Age of Revolution*; *The Age of Capital 1848-1875*; *The Age of Empire*; *The Age of Extremes 1914-1991*.

Hobsbawm coined the terms "long nineteenth" and "short twentieth" centuries and examined the period in these classic four volumes. Very much worth tackling at some point, for instance over the course of a dark, chilly winter.

HOUSLEY, CLIFF/LEIVARS, JUSTIN: *12th (Pioneer) Battalion Sherwood Foresters 1914-1918 with the 24th Division*; Miliquest Publications; Long Eaton. Referenced as: HOU/LEI.

One of the many histories of individual battalions, full of useful information for any researcher looking into the history of the unit or anyone who served in it. Although published sometime in the 2000s or early 2010s, it reads like the battalion histories written around 1920, full of terms like "greatest sacrifice".

SHEFFIELD, GARY (2001): *Forgotten Victory – The First World War: Myths and Realities*; Headline; London. Referenced as: SHE.

A classic work of new revisionism. Undoubtedly important and fascinating, but often infuriating.

SHEFFIELD, GARY/BOURNE, JOHN (eds.; 2006): *Douglas Haig – War Diaries and Letters 1914-1918*; Phoenix; London. Referenced as: SHE/BOU.

A very useful edition of Haig's version of events. Offers intriguing information. Also, it keeps your hatred sharp.

STARLING, JOHN; LEE, IVOR (2009): *No Labour, No Battle – Military Labour during the First World War*; Spellmount; Stroud. Referenced as: STA/LEE.

Not a particularly fun read, but we are thankful to the authors, whose painstaking work produced this very helpful guide to make some sense of the British Army's organisation of their labour force.

You have probably noticed that we did not quite stick to our usual ways of extensive research with primary sources, resulting in an amply referenced and lavishly footnoted text (well, we could not resist including a few of the latter). Nevertheless, amongst the primary evidence we did examine were the following documents and databases:

Records regarding Charles Brett (private, soldier number 20652) retrieved from: ANCESTRY.CO.UK (including documents from the *British Army WWI Service Records*, *British Army WWI Medal Rolls Index Cards*; *WWI Service Medal and Award Rolls*; the databases *UK, Soldiers Died in the Great War* and *UK, Army Registers of Soldiers' Effects*; 1881, 1901, 1911 census records); COMMONWEALTH WAR GRAVES COMMISSION'S casualty database; *The Derby Daily Telegraph* Friday, 22nd October 1915.

COMMONWEALTH WAR GRAVES COMMISSION: *Find War Dead (casualty database)*; www.cwgc.org.

HAMMERTON, JA (ed.; 1920): *Harmsworth's Atlas of the World and Pictorial Gazetteer with an Atlas of the Great War*; The Amalgamated Press; London.

NATIONAL ARCHIVES: *12 Battalion Sherwood Foresters (Pioneers) (Nottinghamshire and Derbyshire Regiment)*; August 1915-May 1919; reference: WO95/2201/1.

NATIONAL ARCHIVES: *Headquarters Branches and Services: General Staff*; September 1915; reference: WO95/158/1.

Assorted articles from the *Nottingham Evening Post*; November 1914, April and May 1915.

The following offer glimpses into some of the everyday experiences of soldiers:

ASHWORTH, TONY (2000): *Trench Warfare 1914-1918 – The Live and Let Live System*; Pan Books; London.

A book on the many ways of combat avoidance and the everyday experiences of trench warfare. Features the best brief summary of the structure of the British Army, the layout of trench systems, etc. we have yet encountered.

BBC: *The Great War Interviews - A collection of interviews with World War One veterans and civilians …*; in: BBC IPLAYER.

FRIEDRICH, ERNST (2014 – originally published 1924): *War against War!*; Spokesman; Nottingham.
To this day this incredible source has not lost any of its impact, documenting the cost of war in haunting images. Contains what governments and militaries (then as now) do not want you to see. If you know anyone who wants to join the army, make them look through this book. All of it.

SMITH, LORENZO N (2014 – originally published 1918): *Lingo of No Man's Land – A World War I Slang Dictionary*; The British Library; London.
If you need to know your Whizz Bangs from your Pill Boxes, these dictionaries are not only very helpful, but in themselves remarkable documents of social history.

WINTER, DENIS (2014 – originally published 1978): *Death's Men – Soldiers of the Great War*; Penguin, London.
This book allows you to follow New Army volunteers on their journey from the recruiting office to the battlefields and back home. An excellent early(ish) example of writing World War One Alltagsgeschichte (roughly translated as everyday history).

Fictionalised accounts by survivors:

REMARQUE, ERICH MARIA (1996 - originally published 1929): *All Quiet on the Western Front*; Vintage; London.
Written by someone who had seen the war and hated it. A brilliant book, as important as it was on the day it was first published.

GRISTWOOD, AD (this edition 2016): *The Somme – Also Including the Coward*; Casemate; Oxford.
Two intriguing short stories about one of the most basic instincts: the urge to stay alive. This makes it even more tragic that the author killed himself in 1933.

Finally, to get a better idea of our general take on World War One as well as many of the subjects mentioned in this book, please have a look at our work regarding death sentences and mutiny convictions against Sherwood Foresters:

http://peopleshistreh.wordpress.com/103-foresters

Excerpts from the 12th Foresters' *War Diary*

The following is a transcript of the 12th Battalion Sherwood Foresters' *War Diary* (WO95/2201/1) for the period August to September 1915. It was recorded by the same hand during those months, but the entries were not signed. The document is rather detailed compared with various other *War Diaries* we studied.

Punctuation and spelling have been partially corrected/modernised and most abbreviations and acronyms spelled out.

Please note that Charlie Brett was transferred on the 5th August from B to A Company (see also his Service Record, available on ANCESTRY.CO.UK).

August 1915		
Chobham Common	21st	Trench Warfare.
Turfhill	22nd	Sunday.
Chobham Common	23rd	Trench Warfare.
	24th	Trench Warfare.
	25th	Trench Warfare.
Aldershot	26th	Musketry-firing on ASH Ranges.
	27th	Company drill, bayonet fighting etc.
	28th	Preparing to embark.
	29th	Entrained at Govt Sidings 6.10 to 8.10am, arrived SOUTHAMPTON 10.15am, embarked at 5pm for HAVRE.
Havre	30th	Disembarked 7am and marched to Camp 2, arrived 11.30am.
	31st	Left Camp No 2 at 8am for GARDE DES MARCHANDISES, and entrained at 1pm.
September 1915		
Hesdin	1st	4am Detrained and marched to LE BIEZ to billets.

September 1915 (continued)		
Le Biez	2nd	Battalion on Kit inspection, fire control and discipline under Company Commanders.
	3rd	Rain all day. Battalion under lecture from Company Officers re Standing Orders etc.
	4th	10am Battalion moved into new billets at ST DENOEUX.
Saint-Denœux	5th	Kit Inspection. Bayonet fighting etc.
	6th	Physical drill etc., 12.15pm moved off to dig trenches under CRE South of HUMBERT.
	7th	Battalion moved off [to] Digging Ground 9am. Digging 10am to 4pm. 2 Officers and 4NCOs proceeded to ST OMER for a MG course. Lt WH Michell and 2/Lt CH Keitley, Sgts Slack, Hammersley, Cpls Fazey [Fagey?] and Lowe.
	8th	10am to 4pm A Company digging trenches and making redoubts [at] pt 125, Old Mill NNW – ½ mile from ST DENOEUX. B C and D Companies at Digging Ground S of HUMBERT.
	9th	Digging as Sept 8th. 4 Officers spent 18hrs in Trenches at LAVENTIE – 4pm 8/9/15 to 10am 9/9/15. Capts H Carpenter GJM Carrie, NG Pearson, 2/Lt S Pentecost.
Saint-Denœux	10th	A and B Companies digging at Old Mill Pt 125. C and D Companies digging S of HUMBERT.
	11th	Battalion digging trenches as Sept 10th. Capt JH Pearson proceeded to WIZERNE for course in bombing. 2 Officers and 4 NCOs returned from St OMER.
	12th	Battalion digging trenches at Old Mill Pt 125 NNW – ½ mile from St DENOEUX. 2/Lt JL Ward proceeded to St OMER for instruction in German bombs and returned the same night. Smoke helmets were practised.
	13th	6.30am Battalion was practising moving, "alarm" sounded.

September 1915 (continued)		
	13th (cont.)	10.15am-4.15pm Battalion bombers under a Corporal from Guards Division were given instruction. Troops practised in magazine charging. MG section at practice with 4 guns. Remainder of Battalion digging as 12th inst. 2/Lt Ward and 2/Lt SM Mohr proceeded to TERDEGHEM for Bomb Instruction for the day.
	14th	9am-4.15pm 128 men (8 per platoon) under special Bomb Instructor. Remainder of Battalion practising magazine loading etc. Inspection of Gas Helmets, and men washing their clothes.
	15th	9am-4.15pm 2/Lt JL Ward and 2/Lt DM Richardson proceeded to the front for 24 hours in the trenches. 128 men were practised in Bombing, ½ A Company on Musketry. Remainder of Battalion digging trenches.
	16th	9am-4.15pm ½ A Company on Musketry till 1pm. ½ B Company on Musketry 1.30pm till 4pm. 128 men on Bombing under 2/Lt JL Ward and Cpl Shotter. Remainder of Battalion digging trenches at the Old Mill. 2/Lt JL Ward and 2/Lt DM Richardson returned from trenches.
	17th	9am-4.15pm ½ B Company on Musketry till 12.30PM. ½ C Company on Musketry from 1.30 to 4.15pm. 64 bombers training under 2/Lt JL Ward all day (16 per Coy), 20 snipers under 2/Lt S Alder all day, Machine Gun section under Lt RDB Woods and 2/Lt DH Richardson all day. Remainder of Battalion digging trenches at Old Mill.
	18th	9am-4.15pm ½ Company on Musketry till 12.30PM. Machine Gun, Bombers and Snipers all training in the morning. ½ D Company on Musketry from 1.30 to 4.15pm. Remainder of Battalion (with Machine Gun, Bombers and Snipers all afternoon) digging trenches all day.

September 1915 (continued)		
	19th	9am to 11am Bomber training under 2/LT JL Ward. Battalion on Inspection, Bayonet Fighting etc. At 11am Battalion spent rest of day washing underclothes and having baths.
	20th	9am to 4.15pm Battalion on route march from 9am to 12.30pm. In the afternoon, ½ D Company on musketry, snipers of B Company under 2/Lt Alder, Bombers and Machine Gun continued their training, remainder of Battalion practising loading magazines and bayonet fighting.
	21st	9am Musketry machine gun sniping etc. [...] Battalion left at 4.30pm and marched all night to RADINGHEM via HUMBERT, St MICHEL PT St MICHEL, MONTEVILLE.
Radinghem	22nd	Rested all day and moved at 6.30pm via BOMY to HAM EN ARTOIS and arrived at 3.30am on the 23rd in bivouacs and billets.
Ham End Artois	23rd	Rested till 6pm when we left for LE CORNET BOURDOIS and arrived at 7.30pm in bivouacs and billets.
Le Cornet Bourdois	24th	Rested till evening and at 6.30pm left via BUSNES for BETHUNE, arrived at 1.30am on the [25]th and men all put in barracks.
Bethune	25th	10.30am left BETHUNE and marched via BEUVRY, SAILLY LA BOURSE to VERMELLERS. Under shellfire at NOYELLES LES VERMELLES at noon. Moved from VERMELLES to X roads SW of LE RUTOIRE and waited for rest of Division to pass, remained there till 4am.
Le Rutoire	26th	Moved due E and held 1st line of English trenches in reserve of 71st Brigade till 11am. Then advanced in reserve of 72nd and 71st Brigades to attack on VENDIN-LE-VIEL. Reached the LOOS-HULLUCH road when 72nd and 71st Brigades retired and left us on the left flank alone, [4.30pm] after waiting for orders for 1½ hours we were compelled to withdraw and to occupy the German trenches till relieved by the Guards at 2am on the 27th. 6 Officers wounded. 5 Other Ranks killed 56 Other Ranks wounded 29 Other Ranks missing.

September 1915 (continued)		
	27th	2am Left trenches and marched to neighbourhood of NOYELLES-LEZ-VERMELLES where we rested. The GOC 24th Division came down to congratulate the Battalion on the fight of the 26th.
Noyelles Les Vermelles	28th	Moved area of bivouacs twice and rested on S side of BETHUNE-LENS road, NE of NOEUX LES MINES [Nœux-les-Mines]. Capt and Hon Major WH Dickins reported died of wounds.
Annequin	29th	9am Moved here from S side of BETHUNE-LENS road and men resting in reserve trenches. 2 Companies sent out to area E of LE RUTOIRE farm to salvage and burial work. Remainder cleaning equipment andc.
	30th	Work of salvage and burial operation carried on by C Company in the morning 15 bodies buried and SAA and some equipment recovered. D Company went up in the afternoon but shellfire was too heavy and they had to return. Remainder of Battalion at kit inspection, bayonet fighting etc.

Soldiers of the 12th Foresters, died in 1915

Information retrieved from the database of the COMMONWEALTH WAR GRAVES COMMISSION.

Name	Age	Died	Rank	Service Number	Additional information
Bateman, James William	17	06/04	Private	21243	Son of W Bateman. Born at Pleasley Hill, Mansfield.
Smith, Randolph Rae	28	09/08	Second Lieutenant		Son of Oliver Smith, of St James Street, Montreal, Canada.
Rogers, William James	41	18/09	Company Sergeant Major	7363	Husband of Florence Rogers, of 15, Redcliffe Street, Sutton-in-Ashfield, Notts.
Barton, Richard John	27	26/09	Private	15150	Son of Harry and Mary Jane Barton, of 136, Southampton Road, Far Cotton, Northampton.
Brett, Charles		26/09	Private	20652	
Clark, Walker	23	26/09	Corporal	16676	Son of Francis and Elizabeth Clark, of Whirlow, Parkhead, Sheffield; husband of Ada Clark, of Greenberry Farm, Langton-on-Swale, Northallerton.
Guy, William	36	26/09	Private	16732	Son of Edward and Caroline Guy; husband of Sarah Ann Hopkinson (formerly Guy), of Main Street, East Bridgford, Nottingham.
Hall, George Edgar	22	26/09	Private	14463	Son of Luke Hall, of 27, Studley Terrace, Cromford Road, Wirksworth, Derbys, and the late Elizabeth Ann Hall.

Name	Age	Died	Rank	Service Number	Additional information
Packer, William		26/09	Company Quarter-master Sergeant	7443	
Roberts, Zachariah Male	30	26/09	Private	17760	Son of Zechariah and Julia Roberts, of 31, Etruria Road, Hanley; husband of Elizabeth Roberts, of 4, Willow Row, High Street, Silverdale, Staffs.
Ryles, George		26/09	Private	14715	
Weston, Samuel	28	26/09	Private	15603	Son of Joseph and Martha Weston, of 139, Crompton Street, New Houghton, Mansfield, Notts.
Dickins, Wyndham Harold	45	28/09	Major		Son of Colonel HF Dickins; husband of Beatrice Dickins, of 2, Belsize Grove, Hampstead, London.
Boden, Hugh Charles Wollaston	19	11/10	Captain		Son of the Reverend CCJ Boden and MLM Boden, of Nuthall Rectory, Nottingham.
Bradwell, George Victor	23	18/10	Private	27059	Son of Thomas and Elizabeth Bradwell.
Watson, H	25	09/11	Private	17079	Son of Wallace and Alice Watson, of Steeton, Yorks.
Biggins, James		17/11	Lance Corporal	18223	
Hine, Thomas	38	25/12	Private	17179	Husband of Ada Hine, of 41, Ossington Street, Radford, Nottingham.

Bluebell Hill Boy

The sparks were shooting out of the bedroom door, dropping onto our nightwear. Dad rushed us all downstairs, mum hid under the table and then ran off. When she was found later in an air raid shelter on Flewitt Street, she was very distressed.

The year was 1941, the night of the 8th to the 9th May. It is said that the earliest in most people's lives that they can remember are events from around four or five years old. Unless something really dramatic happened to them earlier, then some can remember. The above "door in flames" incident is still imprinted in my memory at the ripe old age of seventy-eight. I was two years and ten months old at the time.

On that night a hundred German bombers dropped their death-dealing cargo onto the city of Nottingham. High explosives and incendiary bombs hit houses all over the city, especially in the Meadows, St Ann's, Sneinton, Leenside and Carlton. Our house, 18 Crown Street, just off Bluebell Hill Road, was one of the unfortunate ones hit. One hundred and fifty-one folk lost their lives that night, but we Bretts at number 18 were lucky. Although the incendiary bomb tore through the slate roof, crashed through the bedroom ceiling and ignited the door leading onto the landing, none of the five of us suffered any physical injury. We were damned lucky.

The base of this bomb, about as big as a large tin of baked beans, was used for years afterwards as a flower pot on the scullery windowsill. No doubt my elder sister Eunice, who was nine, put dandelions and such like in it. Why we were not all in the air raid shelter at the time is still a mystery to me.

There were two air raid shelters on Crown Street, and one of them was almost opposite our front door. One night my mother, sister, brother Derek and myself – who by the way owing to my young age was placed in a clothes basket – were all standing half way down the cellar steps. Then in rushed my father with his tin hat on, I believe he was a fire warden of some sorts. "Come on Kit" he said. "Get you and the kids to the shelter, they are coming over again." So with coats on top of our pyjamas we hurried to the safety of the air raid shelter. Many of the residents of our street were inside, and soon my sister Eunice got all our younger kids organised. I remember having to stand up and recite nursery rhymes, baa-baa black sheep etc.

One night a factory or warehouse on the next street, Wright Street, was hit, so a fireman traced hosepipes down our entry, over the back yard and attacked this fire from our back garden. As I watched all this, up in the sky, two aircraft were passing high overhead. The one in front had smoke coming out of it and the other was following close behind. Whether they were German or ours I do not know. Being so young I had no comprehension of what this war was all about, it was just a game to me. In fact I must have enjoyed being woken in the night and rushed off to the shelters. My observations of these two aircraft was soon interrupted by my ten year old brother Derek grabbing me and hustling me inside.

My father received the first of his so-called "war wounds" when he attempted to get a Mrs Fulbrook out of her house at number eleven. Her front door was locked, and I believe she didn't want to come out. So dad took a few steps back, but soon met the shelter wall, he took a short run towards the door, but when he ascended the two steps he had lost all his momentum. With his shoulder he hit the door and bounced back down the steps smashing into the air raid shelter wall.

His other wound was later on in the war, when he was called up at the age of forty-three. Whilst in the Far East he was accidentally grabbed by a ship's crane. He was hospitalised and never fully recovered from this as far as I can tell, for he suffered many years of agony with one of his kidneys, finally having to have it removed.

The last event I can remember of the war was when my mother took me to a place at the bottom of Sneinton Dale to get my gas mask. Being so young and little it was not the familiar face gas mask for me, I got the Mickey Mouse one. It was red and I had to sit or lay in it and be zipped up from the outside. I can still remember the horrible rubbery smell that it gave off.

I don't know what year, but my brother took me to Colwick Woods on the 44 trolley bus, catching it just outside Victoria Park on Bath Street. Just over the railway crossing there was a compound holding some

Italian prisoners of war. For a couple of cigarettes these prisoners would make a toy. One such toy was four ducks on a flat piece of wood about eight inches square. By pulling some string all the ducks nodded their heads and made a tapping noise. I myself never got one, I was too young to know where to get cigarettes.

At last VE Day came. Not really knowing what it was all about it didn't take me long to get into the swing of things. Trestles and forms filled all the streets, triangular cut potted meat sandwiches, ice cream and even lemonade and Tizer. Even today whenever I see triangular cut sandwiches I think of VE Day. That same night bonfires were lit all over the place and the adults left the many pubs in this area singing and dancing.

I returned to Colwick Woods in 2002, and wished I hadn't.

In my days in the late 1940s, one took a jam jar back to Ada Wright's shop on Flewitt Street. That got you two pence, ample for the two way bus fare. On arrival at the Colwick bus terminus, one was instantly transported into another world. Totally different from the narrow cobbled streets and the back to back houses we all lived in. Not a building in sight, and you could even hear the birds singing. Through the rickety iron gate, turn right and straight uphill to what we called dark wood. Now it was Cowboys and Indians. When we got bored with that it was onwards deeper into this vast wood till eventually we arrived at the swamp. A dell that was always soggy as a spring came out of a pipe jutting out of the bank side, quenching our thirst. It was now time to play Tarzan on the thick rope hanging from a tree. Time now to go home, and what a sight we must have looked in our short trousers, mudded up, our face and hands absolutely filthy. Back at the 44 terminus the poles connected to the overhead wires had come off, and the bus conductor had to pull out a very long connecting pole to get the bus reconnected. Happy days.

Now look at Colwick Woods, buildings all around including a tower block, dirty looking factory yards, graffiti, and the endless noise of traffic.

It came at last, my first day at school. This was to be Bluebell Hill Infants' School, only about hundred yards from my house. A Miss Alders greeted me and told me to put my packed lunch in a wicker basket with all the other kids' lunches. After what seemed a year, the time for playtime bell rang, so off with about twenty others we joined the throng of kids out in the playground. Now in this yard there was a low wall that led to Beacon Hill, a steep short road leading to Crown Street. Thinking my school career had finished, I hopped over this wall and legged it back home, down the entry and through the back door into the scullery. Mam was doing some washing. I tried to explain to her that school had finished.

On listening to this she said: "You've a long time to go yet me lad till your school days are over, you've got years yet. Come on." She grabbed me by the collar and frog marched me back to school. From that day on the teacher on playground duty closely watched me. Miss Alders was a lovely teacher and I still have fond memories of her. One day my mother visited her, I could see them talking, and I knew that they were discussing me. Eventually mother left and Miss Alders came immediately to my desk and removed all my coloured chalks leaving me with only white. It appeared that I was fond of eating and chewing them. Mary Basset who sat next to me gave me a smirky look, so at playtime I gave her a thump.

June Baker was running around the playground and everybody was chasing her. What could it be? She was eating something as she ran along, and this something was a banana. Now I had never seen a banana before, and neither had any of the other boys and girls. After scoffing it down her she threw the skin high up into the air. Then there was a mad tussle as the screaming mob ripped this skin to pieces and ate it. I too joined in but sadly got none of it.

I had never tasted or seen a tomato either, so was curious one day when I espied on the sideboard a tin that said on it tomato juice. I can still remember the name on it. It said Cirio Tomato Juice, and had a picture of a cocktail glass filled with red liquid and a drinking straw. I approached and touched this strange object. My mum's voice rang out: "Leave it be, it's for a special occasion."

That special occasion came when my Father was demobbed from the army. For on the next Sunday morning we all sat down to dried eggs, bacon and lovely tomato juice. It was indeed a feast. I hadn't missed my father going into the army, as I was too young to really know him when he was called up.

I must have wondered who this man was that had entered our lives. I accepted his gifts though. He gave me a box full of wooden blocks with pictures on all sides of eyes, noses, mouths etc. By juggling them around one could make numerous faces. Indeed the toy was called "the man with a thousand faces". My sister and brother got three dimensional wooden jigsaw puzzles including a cube, an elephant and Tower Bridge. What my mother got I didn't know as I was too busy playing with my new toy. I was really proud anyhow of him when he took me to school one morning, for he let me wear his army jungle hat, a bit like a cowboy hat and the one Australian soldiers wear.

I was chuffed, as they say, parading around the playground with it on. The toys and the hat are now sadly gone, but what we still have in the family are one or two of what we call Chinese boxes. Dad told us that for one or two small coins, street carve traders in Hong Kong would carve for you these boxes. I keep all my important documents in the one I still have, although the unusual key system has been lost over the years.

So over the months, things started to get back as near to normal. Rationing was still on and mum spent hours at Ada Wright's shop on a Saturday getting our provisions. The men were home and the pubs again were full. There were plenty of them in our area. Robin Hood, Blue Bell, Alfred, Victory, Hop Bloom, Bath Inn, Colin Campbell, White Lion, to mention just a few. Shops also were many and very near. I remember Spickes the beeroff, Marriots the toffee shop, Bywaters newsagents, Russells on Flewitt Street, Riley's fish and chip shop, Curtis's, Oswins for wet fish, Cotteralls dairy shop and a Co-op to name a few.

Funny but I can remember many events in infant school, but hardly anything at all about my sojourn in Bluebell juniors.

However I do remember a Miss Morris and a Miss Castle. Now Miss Castle's face was plastered with thick white face powder, she looked hideous and I thought she was at least a hundred years old. Older kids told us that if you did anything wrong Miss Morris would rap the back of your thighs with a ruler.

I must admit though that I never saw her do it to anyone.

Years after when my mother lived at Carlton, I drove her to see all of what remains of Bluebell Hill Infant and Junior School. As a monument to the past, the council left the opening archway to the school. It was however sadly removed a few years ago. Mother looked around, but seemed confused, couldn't get her bearings. We then wandered some short distance to where I believed our old house stood. Again what with all the new housing developments back in the 1960s, mum was a little baffled and confused. As with my trip to Colwick Woods in later life, I have come to realise that one should keep one's memories in one's head, and not try to re-capture them by visiting past sites of your youth. Standing there near to where number 18 Crown Street once stood I looked at mum and gave out a little laugh and smile. When she asked me what I was smiling at, I told her that I had just remembered an embarrassing event when I was about three. So I told her. Trying to toilet train me one day, mum had took my short trousers off and told me it was time I went to the loo myself. Now I could hear my sister and some of her friends playing in the next-door neighbour's back yard. It was a good ten yards or so to our outdoor toilet, and though only about three years old I was conscious of my body parts, but mum insisted, so I ran like the devil. I don't suppose that my sister and her female friends even noticed me, as they were too intent on their play. On telling this tale to my mother, she laughed, which was very rare for her, and said: "Geroff ya daft bogger."

There was no TV in those days, so we kids had to make our own amusements, and we were all very good at this. Street games came in many forms, some of them were seasonal, only done at certain times of the year. I liked Tin Lurky, where one of the team threw an empty tin down the street as far as they could. The seeker had to then run after the tin, pick it up and bring it back and place it in the centre of the road. Whilst they did this the rest of the mob went and hid in the many, many hiding places that abounded in districts like this. Sometimes I cheated, and instead of hiding used to go home and listen to the radio. Other games were Dobby on Step, Sly Fox, Dog and Bone. The boys mostly played marbles, a hole in the cobblestones was called the "choc" and a red blood alley marble was the most coveted of possessions. Whip and top was seasonal, we put chalk patterns on their tops, and carrot tops and window breakers were our favourite models of these spinning objects. Girls played hopscotch, skipping, ball-juggling and doing handstands against the wall, their dresses tucked into their knickers for this event. Skipping consisted of Under the Moon and Over the Stars, and very fast skipping was done to various songs, Salt-Mustard-Vinegar-Pepper etc. We young lads would often use our mother's sweeping brush as a horse when we played Cowboys and Indians. Trailing it between our legs we gave our backsides a hit and off we galloped attacking the enemy.

I would sit for hours with two or three others on Mr Hill's low front wall, we all had balaclavas on pretending to be bomber pilots, "brum, brum, brum brum" the droning sound of a bomber plane. It must have driven the Hills mad, for many a time he would come out and tell us to piss off round our own houses. This we probably did, and thought no more of it, unlike today when you could half expect a brick through your window.

The only way to make money in those days was to run errands for folk. Mrs Age, who lived next door to us, gave you a penny if you went to Spicky's the beeroff for her. Normally it was for a pint of Shippo's mild in a jug, at other times you had to take a cup and ask for Indian Brandy. I wasn't always honest with Mrs Age. With a white basin I was supposed to go all the way down Alfred Street to a certain butchers to get some dripping for her, only this butchers' produce would do for her. I wasn't having that, it was a long way off, so getting the dripping from a nearby butchers I played for about fifteen minutes with mates on Flewitt Street, returning then to get my penny. She never twigged on.

At 5.45 each night, not a lad was to be seen on the street. It was *Dick Barton – Special Agent* on our Rediffusion wireless, with his partners, Snowy and Jock. Then we all rushed out and re-enacted what we had just heard. Another play I can remember was *Lady in the Fog* by Philip Odell – yes I can still remember that name. *Paul Temple* was another favourite. It used to end something like this: "Paul, there's something touching my shoulder." Then the music started, the tune *Coronation Scott*, one of my favourites still.

Saturday was well looked forward to. It was down the hill to Riley's fish shop. Now Mr Riley was one huge man, yet his wife couldn't have been more than four foot and six inches. Riley's chips were like most chips in those days, crispy and golden brown, not like the pasty-faced yellow ones you get nowadays. Once back home with the goodies we all listened to Tommy Handley's *ITMA* (*It's That Man Again*). I can still remember some of the characters and one-liners. "Can I do you now sir?" and the ex-army officer saying. "A scotch! I don't mind if I do." Then there was *Round the Horne.*

This wireless we had also gave me my love for classical music. For my father used it for his alarm clock. You see the radio programmes went off the air at about midnight, and didn't come on again until about seven in the morning. So my poor mother especially had to endure this late music whilst in bed until it went off. From it I got my love for Elgar, Holst, Chopin, Ravel, and especially Beethoven and Tchaikovsky. Father also introduced me to another love of my life, chess. He had made a set out of beer bottle tops I believe and cardboard. Once I had mastered the basics I soon improved, so much that in my secondary school days at Manvers, I became the school's chess club captain. I can remember once beating Huntingdon School (Hunto our arch enemy) 7-0. But a bigger scalp we got was when we won High Pavement Grammar School. We looked at the pupils from this school as sissies, all smart in their expensive uniforms. I don't think they lived in the dwellings we occupied. Yes it was literally class war.

At about the age of six, I had my first date. It was with Jeany Calcroft from number 14. So off our gang went to play on King Edwards Park at the bottom of Carlton Road on the swings and the slide, then we all sat down on the grass. Suddenly Jean stood up saying: "I don't want to go out with you no more," and ran off! Ah well, so much for lost love. I often see Jean still when I bump into her at the Clifton shops.

I also got my first feeling of guilt at about this age. Home from school for the dinner break, I kept pestering my mother for some money. She refused saying she had not got any money to spare, which was probably true. However I still persisted until she got really angry. Knowing the mood she was in I scarpered out the door, up the entry and made my way back to school.

The front door opened. "Here Colin, take this." I gingerly crept back and she thrust a sixpenny piece in my hand. Although glad of this I somehow knew that she couldn't afford it, but I spent it all the same.

I have three more recollections of my early boyhood before I give memories of when I was a bit older. I was about eight, and it was around Christmas time. So Jean Calcroft, Brenda Dodwell and myself went carol singing. In those days you sang one or two carols before knocking on the door. Not like today where the kids knock on the door first. Well, we did very well this night: we collected 2/6 (or two shillings and sixpence for the ignorant) – half a crown wowee! I was off like a shot with the money. Into Bluebell Post Office, and bought the wind-up train engine that I had seen in the window for months. Playing with it in my play area near the cellar step door, I heard a knock. Mother opened the door and in stepped Mrs Calcroft and Mrs Dodwell. Words were exchanged. When they left mum took the engine off me, clipped me round the ear and kicked me off to bed. "Wait till your dad comes home me lad." Mum often used to say those words to me, yet dad on coming home never gave me any more punishment. Neither can I ever remember him ever hitting me. He was a good sort.

Some Canadian soldiers once visited our school and left hundreds of small tins filled with all sorts of goodies. There were Horlick's tablets, chocolate powder, some sweets and a small packet of sugar. We probably made ourselves sick. What fun.

I was walking by Andersons, the pawnbroker's shop on St Ann's Well Road one day when a woman carrying a bundle stopped me and said. "Hey up duck, if you take this parcel in here I will give you a tanner."

Now a tanner is not to be sneezed at, so into Andersons the pawnbrokers I did go. I can't remember what was in the parcel, but he gave me some money, so off I trotted outside and gave this cash to the woman. She thanked me, gave me the sixpence and I ambled home a happy lad. On telling mum my good fortune, she hit the ceiling. "Jesus Christ" she screamed, "did anyone we know see you go in?" I shook my head. "No." "Are you sure, are you sure? What will people say if they think we are that bad off. Now look here my lad, never go in that shop again, you hear me?" I didn't know what all the fuss was about at the time, but kept my promise and never went there again.

Finally I reached the good old age of ten. I could venture further afield now, seek out new pastures and kingdoms. All the kids went to Saturday morning pictures. I joined the one at the Empress Cinema. Uncle Mac ran it, and when you joined you had to fill in your birthday. So with prior knowledge from elder members, you always put your birthday just about two weeks away. The reason being that you got in for nothing that week and also got an orange. You couldn't hear a damn thing at these Saturday rushes as all the kids booed when the villain appeared on the screen, then whistled and cheered when the hero came on the scene to save the damsel in distress. Hopalong Cassidy, Roy Rogers, Lone Ranger, Gene Autry were our heroes, the bad lads being Peg Leg, and One Eyed Jack, just to name two.

On the next few pages I will list the names of people on Crown Street that I remember, and a few who lived elsewhere. Perhaps in the future someone will read the names and capture a bit of the past.

On the odd number side of the street at the bottom corner stood Spicky's the beeroff. Now he was strange character. Nearly always drunk, he would bite your head off if you asked him to change a sixpence into pennies for the gas meter. We got our own back on him many times though by climbing over his back wall, with broken glass cemented on the top, nicked a few of his empties (empty beer bottles), then took them to other shops to get a penny on the bottle. Some of the gang even took them back to Spicky's himself!

At number 1 was Mr Thompson, his wife and son Jimmy who was about my age. Now Mr T was in his youth handy in the boxing ring. This is no surprise as the Thompsons were closely related to Bendigo, Nottingham's most famous boxer, who is buried in Bath Street cemetery. Next to them at the corner of Beacon Hill was an elderly woman named Smith, she was always out telling us off for the noise we were making. The Hills lived at 5, I think he was a builder, and they kept very much to themselves. Now their daughter Gloria was a good-looking lass, knew how to dress proper and loved dancing, singing, acting etc. I once saw her in a show at the Arboretum. We young kids were very wary when we went to the Arboretum as in that area lived "black folk" and we walked quickly by their houses if they were standing outside.

At 7 lived Jack and Lillian Plaskett, with their children Barbara and David. A lodger also named Jack lived with them. I believe he came originally from London. At 9 were the Wightmans, Walter and wife Sarah. They had many kids. Dennis, Barry, Ronnie, Raymond, David, Brian, and daughter Pauline. How they all squeezed into that tiny house is beyond me. At number 11 was a woman called Phyllis, I can't say much about her at all. Now at 13 lived Mrs Fullbrook with daughter Sheila and son Frankie. Sheila was not a healthy girl and died whilst still young.

To get to the next two houses one had to go through an enclosed passageway. The Daniels lived in one of those (another family who kept to themselves). I believe that he was a bus driver or conductor. Further down on the odd side of Crown Street lived the Parson family. Next came the Disneys. The father worked down the pit. His sons were Brian and Colin (one of my mates). Now we come to Mr and Mrs Simmons. Now these two were an odd pair. On many occasions after leaving the pubs they would break out into an ear splitting row that could be heard all over the street. On most of these noisy rows, Mr Simmons would lock the doors and not let her in. She stood outside for hours cursing him. Yes, a strange couple.

The Dodwells lived next door to them. He was an ex sailor and had a window cleaning round. If memory serves me right he did a few weeks in the nick for buying some ladders he knew to be stolen. Their daughter Brenda I have told you about in my Xmas carol fiasco. A son named Keith rounded off this family. Then came the Parsons and next the Dales. Now the Dales of Nottingham are a large family indeed, and once you have seen one Dale, you have seen them all. They all have the same characteristic face details. Bill my best mate lived here. Poor Bill, he never really had the best of health. In later life he married and moved up to Clifton, had one of his legs amputated and died at a very early age in life. He had a brother named Gordon. Next door lived the Harolds. Mr Harold rode a motorbike with sidecar. He had a false leg, losing it in World War One. I didn't get on at all well with his son, Derek I believe was his name. A lot older than me I steered well clear of him. Mr Harold's daughter I believe was named Ena. She was one of my sister's best friends, always at our house cutting and sticking film star pictures into scrapbooks etc.

Now we cross over the street to our side, the even number side. On the bottom corner was Marriots the toffee shop. He sold delicious ice cream. Later in my teens I was buying a Raleigh cycle on the weekly. Not yet used to the set up on this machine, I pulled on the gear lever instead of the brake. I careered right through his shop door and finished up in a crumpled heap near the ice cream counter. Picking my bruised body up, I cheekily said: "A choc ice please!" I can't remember his reply, but it wasn't very cordial I can tell you.

At number one I believe lived Mr Croft, he worked on the dustbins. One of his sons, Jimmy was a right rogue. A lot older than myself, I have seen our Jimmy fighting not only with the Cavendish cinema manager, but also with the coppers when they arrived on the scene. Yes Jimmy Croft was a right handful in his youth. I often wondered if he settled down in later life. I think he did.

Now we come to the Browns. I don't know much about this family only that they all had light kind of ginger hair and freckles. The Reads lived near them. She made wreaths and crosses and organised the distribution of the lace that many of the women did around there to supplement their income. In fact I have done a bit of lace ripping in my time helping my mother out. Thousands of bits of cotton lace covered the carpets and rugs when this operation was being done. There were no hoovers in those days.

Getting closer to our house now, at number 12 lived a dear elderly couple called Mr and Mrs Comery. I think they were related to the Plasketts. A number of families lived in that house when they passed away.

First to move in were the Poxen family. These became very great friends of my mother. Ken was a lot older than me, as was Barry. Then there was a daughter, Kathleen I believe, who was mates with my sister Eunice. When they moved out the Browns occupied number 12. Sheila, their youngest daughter, was roughly my age, and as we grew into our middle teens all the lads were after her. The older daughter Lillian later on married Ray Whitman from across the street. I have often seen them out shopping together up here in Clifton.

At 14 was the Calcroft family. Bill worked at Raleigh I think, and you never saw him without his blue overalls on. A big man was Bill Calcroft. His wife Florrie, though called Flo, was a very thin woman and also a close friend of our family. She shopped at the

Co-op, and often gave us a big chocolate sponge cake. Flo, who was born in Canada, had three children. Bill, Barbara and Jean. On certain nights we all played the horse racing game called Totopoly at Bill's house. This game (much better than Monopoly) passed away many a happy hour. In 2001 I saw this game at a car boot site in Derbyshire, so I bought it for a few quid. It was great to see the names of some of the horses again that I couldn't remember after all those years. But there they were. Dorado, Marmaduke Jinks, Dark Warrior, Flamenco etc. I could go on but won't bore you.

Next door to us across the entry was the aged Gramma Plaskett. Sometimes a Peter and a Dave Plaskett came to live with her. Dave and I spent years together growing up. A handsome lad was he with dark black curly hair. All the girls fell for him, and I must admit I was a little bit jealous of him, yet we were big pals. He later married Sheila Austin, who lived up Beacon Hill. Both moved up North, and I have neither seen nor heard from them ever since.

On the other side of us lived another old lady with the apt name of Mrs Age. She had the only bit of garden on our block that had plants growing on it. But woe betide anyone if she saw you trespassing on it. She had a very large pure white cat called Snowy. Sometimes I used to lock it in her toilet, and I had great fun listening to her shout Snowy in for its dinner.

Next came Mrs Crow, another old lady living on her own. She often came out and chased us away to go and play elsewhere. Then there was Lotty (or Lottie?).

This very hard working woman was very small and always wore a green wraparound apron. Her face was all wrinkled and she always had a hair net on. But our Lotty was the scourge of the street when it came to us lads. I'm sure that if a fly passed by her window, she would be out like a shot to see what the noise was. Many a time she would come running out with a sweeping brush, waving it threateningly at us shouting. "Geroff you cheeky young bleeders, piss off round yer own end, now geroff." Know what? We did just that. Didn't want a swipe of Lotty's broom when she was in that mood I can tell you.

Further down the street near Flewitt Street lived another of my best mates. Michael O'Brian. Mick's mum was Irish and also had two daughters, Sheila and Kathleen. They seemed very poor, even to my young eyes. Kathleen was a very sickly young girl, always ill and in bed. It was no surprise when one day she died, and the whole street turned out for her funeral. Later when the mother died, the Dykes who lived a few doors away took in poor Mick. Although it was very good of them to do so, it made Mick's life very unhappy.

I think they were too old to take Mick on. Not only that but they were very strict with him. The poor lad couldn't take comics into the house, nor eat anything whilst on the street. He was called in at the first sign of any noise. Mrs Dykes didn't like me at all, in fact I don't think she liked him playing with anybody. On top of all that he went to the Catholic school on Hunt

Street. We had all heard how terrible the nuns were in that place. Perhaps that's why when he reached his late teens he joined up for nine years in the army. I heard years later that he was most successful at this, reaching a very high rank and signed on for the whole twenty-one year contract.

Well that's our street done. Yet just a few more characters are in my memory banks that did not live on our street: Kipperfeet and Lol come to mind. What a name, Kipperfeet! This thin gangly woman used to come flopping up our street in slippers that looked 10 sizes too big for her. Hence her nickname. Her son Lol was a very tall lad, walked around similar to his mother. He always wore a large bib overall. Muttering and shouting to himself and anyone who crossed his path. Nobody could understand what he was trying to say. This harmless though feeble-minded lad lived on Flewitt Street I believe. Simple minded though he was, I never saw anyone taking the micky out of him. Poor old Lol.

Another character was Kenny. He lived with a kind of businesswoman called Mrs Stokes on Bluebell Hill Road. She had a wood chopping and bundling machine, selling her firewood bundles to local shops. He looked like he had never washed, his face was black. He too would rant on, but at least you could understand him.

Mum and Miss Alders soon got me into reading. One winter's night, mum seeing that I was bored said. "Look in the cupboard, there's something for you."

That something was four small books, *Treasure Island* and *Kidnapped* among the titles. I happily read them until it was time for bed. Dad read the *Mirror*, and I couldn't wait for him to put it down so that I could read the comic strips page. Garth and his friend Prof Lumiere, Buck Ryan, Belinda, Ruggles, and Useless Eustice. If dad saw me looking at him reading, he would often take out the comic page, handing it to me saying. "Give it me back in one piece, I haven't read it myself yet." I always cut Garth out, coloured it in with crayons (I didn't eat crayons any more) and stuck it in a scrapbook using flour and water for the paste.

On Alfred Street was a second hand bookshop, and for tuppence you could swap and get another book or magazine. Dad and I often went, he liked westerns whilst I went in for science fiction, thus discovering my second love in life. As I got older I discovered the writings of world famous authors like Isaac Asimov, Pohl Anderson etc. The public library was at the bottom corner of St Mathias Road, and the female librarian was very strict. Yet in time, seeing my enthusiasm for reading, she let me use the adult section. I can't think of any other young boy she gave this privilege to.

For some time however, I was confused with certain words that were abbreviated, for instance, "bros" and "ltd" got me puzzled, as did the "ampersand".

My love for books has never diminished, for hundreds of them line my bedroom walls today, and I would rather read a good book than watch the nonsense that is on TV today.

Every Wednesday mum with an old pram took the family washing to Victoria baths washhouse. She would be there for hours. Always in a wraparound apron, she then faced ironing the whole lot with a hot iron heated up upon the gas stove, spitting on it occasionally to see if it was hot enough.

About the only time I ever saw her without that apron was Christmas time. Now that was an event any young lad in the late 1940s looked forward to. Different for me today, as I am totally against all religions and haven't celebrated Christmas for the last thirty years or so. Yes Christmas was exciting. For one thing we could use the parlour. Now our parlour was hallowed ground all the year round. Mum had her best furniture in there, a brown leather settee, a china cabinet filled with the best crockery and better quality rugs and carpets than in the living room. A fire would be lit, and we would all spend a happy festival in the parlour until it was shut down again, and out of bounds so to speak for another year. Mum didn't smoke, but always lit one up on Christmas day, and it was comical to see the way she held it puffing away at it. Just as the front parlour was hallowed ground, so was my parent's bedroom. The only time allowed in was if one of my parents was ill in bed and Christmas morning. At around 5am on that morning I would peek around their door and say: "Has he been yet?" The reply would be something like: "No, he hasn't been yet, go back to bed." After two to three enquiries of this nature, I would be told he had arrived. So into mum's wardrobe I did go, to find out what Santa had left me. Magical moments, magical memories.

Another seasonal event was local election time. Mr Cotteral who owned a dairy shop on Bluebell Hill was a Liberal Party man. So with placards nailed onto a stick, hordes of us kids would parade and chant all over the district:

"Vote, vote, vote for Mr Cotteral
You can't vote for a better man
Mr Cotteral is our man
And we'll have him if we can
And we won't come knocking on your door."

We heard that kids down on Roden Street were doing the same thing, but for a different candidate. This was war! So off we would charge and battle commenced. We followed the slow moving election cars and vans with their loudspeakers, urging the people to come out and vote, and offering anyone a lift to the polling booths if they needed transport. Voting took place at my school, so it was a day's holiday for us young ones.

Conker collecting and scrumping too were seasonal occupations. The conkers were found up the Wells Road, and by lobbing half bricks at the high branches, we brought them tumbling to the ground. Then these conkers were put through many secretive scientific processes. These secrets were handed down over the generations from one friend to another. Wrapping them in brown paper and placing them in a dark cupboard was one way. Another was pickling them in vinegar for a day or two. Better than conkers was scrumping. Most of my scrumping with the Crown Street gang was up near the mounts. That was up via Gordon Road, Thornywood Mount and then across Porchester Road and down into the fields of Mapperly Plains.

Mapperly Plains is now one huge built up area. In fact no more plains exist. In my day when one went there it was like the American prairies to me. Vast open land as far as the eye could see. We did our grasshopper collecting here as well as frog catching, newts for our jam jar aquariums, and best of all scrumping for delicious Russet apples. Nothing tasted better than these Russets, and one cannot find them anywhere in the shops nowadays. On a bad day though it was usually crab-apples. Then eating them like pigs we all suffered stomach pains and running to the toilet. Bliss. Near Mounts was an old disused brickyard. Had to be careful here! Or "Choc" would get you. I don't know who this Choc was, nor whether he was a man or boy, if he ever existed that is. Yet on seeing some distant figure approaching, the cry would go up: "Chock!" and we would all run like mad. For we heard he did terrible things to you if caught.

Pads was another adventurous place to explore. This old brickyard I believe, was between Carlton Road and Sneinton Dale. It was also a short cut when one went to the Saturday morning cinema on the dale.

One activity I didn't get on too well with was boxing. In fact my career in this sport lasted no more than one round. Wally Swift was a well-known local boxer and lived around the corner from us on Bluebell Hill. He had opened up a boxing club for the young ones in the area. On my first night's attendance at this venue, Wally was too busy with other things. So said to me. "Put some gloves on and, now let me see, ha yes, have a few rounds with Kenny." Now Kenny I knew. About a year younger than me, I knew I could beat him in a street fight any day. So in the ring I jumped assured of winning him. What a mistake. There are rules in boxing not in street fighting. He punched me from pillar to post. After about five minutes of this I had had enough. It was off gloves then off home at a rapid rate of knots. I had more respect for Kenny after that.

Whenever our teachers mentioned the words Rose Hill clinic, we shuddered in fear. For that meant only one thing. Injections. The dreaded needle. Also at this clinic we had to go sometimes to have our scabs and wounds treated. The remedy was always the same. Purple lotion painted on the parts infected. We came out of the clinic painted up like Apaches going on the warpath. Also in the same area was Rose Hill School. This school was for – how can I say? For kids not too bright. One lad from our street attended this school, David Boulter. He was about a year younger than me, but my what a size he was. Not many tangled with big Dave. Yet I was informed later on in life that when he was born, he was that tiny that they had to wrap him up in cotton wool and place him in a large jug of some sorts. True or not I don't know. I remember David as a big gangly lad always with a runny nose and sniffling it back all the time.

One delight for me was when we visited Aunt Ada. She lived in a council house on Skipton Circus just off Sneinton Dale. It was a different world up there. A front gate as well as a front garden. The back garden was very long, and Uncle Ernest kept a few hens for the eggs and no doubt for Christmas dinner. Yet the most amazing thing about Aunt Ada's house was that it had an indoor toilet and a bathroom as well. Our Aunt Ada was a lovely person, warm hearted generous and kind. She was my father's half-sister. Her husband, big Ernest was a bricklayer like my father, he worked at Boots. A sideline he had was a second-hand bookstall on Loughborough market on a Saturday. When he sometimes visited us, he would slip dad a brown paper bag. This passing of the bag was done very discreetly. What could it be?

It turned out to be books about a New York detective, who also liked his women. So on certain pages his sexual encounters were described. That was the reason for the discreet passing of the books. Compared with what you can read and see on TV nowadays, Hank Janson books are tame. Yet I suppose they were considered hot stuff in those days.

Aunt Ada had a lovely clean home, and her gardens well groomed. So it was a shock for me when in 1990 I went up to visit her on Skipton Circus. She had moved to a warden aided flat down Colwick Road. The shock being not that she had moved, but the state of the whole area. Boarded up windows, some smashed, gardens unkempt, rubbish everywhere, and the odd burnt out car.

Even today in this too fast a pace of life, Sunday is not Sunday to me unless I have the traditional English Sunday dinner. Roast beef, stuffing, Yorkshire pudding, roast spuds, boiled potatoes, and Bisto gravy. Just like mum cooked. Like all mothers in those days, they had to know how to cook. No fast foods or supermarkets in those days. Steam puddings were one of my favourites, especially spotted dick. Then there was Irish stew. I have tried to do this myself sometimes, but it never comes out like mum made it.

Yet there was a golden rule at 18 Crown Street. We didn't start eating it until dad came home from the pub. Then we all had an eggcup full of brown ale to wash our dinner down. If he arrived home late this often caused friction between my parents. Then we would all suffer. For whenever they had a row, mother wouldn't even speak to us children. This could go on for days sometimes. She would slap our teas on the table saying: "There take it or leave it, I don't care, I'm just a skivvy around here."

These rowing episodes are about the only bad things I can remember from my early life. My mother was a good clean woman, always kept us well fed, and our clothes were a lot better than some on the street. I hardly ever saw her smile though, and laughing even less. She was a born worrier. I shouldn't really say it, but mum would worry because she had nothing to worry about.

Usually after his Sunday dinner dad went off to bed, and mum kicked us off to Sunday school. It did me no good however because I turned out to be a complete atheist.

Now for a lighter subject. Skeggy!

Yes, the only way for Nottingham folk to spell it. Mr Cotteral our dairyman used to organise day trips to Skeggy and sometimes Mablethorpe. You paid in so much a week to get on these outings. Most of the street went on these seaside trips, and sometimes more than one bus was needed. What delighted us young ones were seeing buses come into our area, it was indeed a rare sight. All aboard, and we were off for the thousand-mile trip to Skeggy, or so we thought. Soon Halfway House was reached. A rush to the toilets, grab a cup of tea, make haste the bus goes in five minutes! All aboard and off we go again.

Who would be the first to see Lincoln cathedral? There it is, and then it was up the very steep Lincoln Hill in the centre of the city. At last our destination is reached, Skeggy. We now had about seven hours to dig up all the sand on the beach, have a paddle in the sea and become racing jockeys on the donkeys. Have our photo taken by Wrates photographers on the prom, then later queue at their office at the beginning of the pier to buy the photos. Fish and chips rounded off a brilliant day.

It was exciting to write that last piece, but more exciting for us when we were young and went on those rare trips. With nearly everyone nowadays having cars, owning caravans, and being able to afford bed and breakfast digs or even hotels, I firmly believe that we enjoyed those trips a hundred times better than today's youngsters. It was the rarity of the event that made it so exciting. The anticipation waiting for the big day.

Still on the Skeggy theme I have two more tales of that seaside resort. After a medical at school, my mother received a letter saying I could go to Skegness for three whole weeks. Another two lads from my class could also go. They were Barry Bell and David Brodell. The three of us were very small for our ages, and I think that one of the reasons was to try and fatten us up a bit, give us lots of fresh air and generally put something back in us that was lacking. A brilliant holiday it was too. No lessons, just playing on the beach. We marched to the cinema each week, and also to the church.

What I didn't like however was bath nights! Then burly women came in with red rubber aprons on and made sure we had a good bath. They didn't miss behind my ears or anywhere else I can tell you. Then it was straight into bed, and a warden came round with hot drinks and potted meat sandwiches. Lights out: "No noise lads, goodnight." Then a chorus of fifty odd lads: "Goodnight sir."

Happy, oh happy days.

My last memory trip to Skegness was in the late forties. Dad had booked for a week at Winthorpe in a caravan. The owner of the caravan said he would take us and bring us back.

Most of the street turned out when the car pulled up. Now this car was big, an American car. Nobody owned a car on our street and to see one on Crown Street was a rare sight. But to see a huge American car, now that was really something. Big though this car was, we were packed in like sardines in a tin. The reason being that another family was also travelling with him to Skegness. I guess he owned more than one caravan. I distinctly remember three things about this week's holiday. Dad had to take a large empty gas cylinder to the front office to get a full one. The empty cylinder was heavy, but dad said the full one would be lighter as it would be full of gas. Well as you know the gas inside is in liquid form and a lot heavier than an empty one, a lot heavier. Laugh, we couldn't stop laughing. Dad had to roll it back to our caravan.

On this holiday I had a septic thumb, and would let no one touch it. My parents and my older brother and sister must have been getting fed up at all this, so they devised a cunning plan. Dad leaned down on one knee in front of me, said in a caring trusting voice. "Look Colin lad, just open your hand and let me just look at it, I promise not to touch it." After a few minutes of deliberation I slowly and warily opened up my hand to let him see. Immediately Derek my brother, who was behind me, grabbed my wrist. Mother slapped on some hot Kaolin poultice and wrapped my thumb up in a bandage. I struggled but it was all over in a flash. They had planned it well.

The last memory of this holiday was brother Derek getting a smack in the tab for cheating at cards, pontoon in fact. Mum and dad went for a drink in the Royal Oak. Leaving the eldest Derek in charge no doubt. The three of us started to play pontoon for pennies. Derek was winning, as he was the banker.

Finally our parents returned. I don't know who spotted it, but it was noticed that Derek who sat opposite my sister Eunice and myself had playing cards on his knees under the table. These cards I believe were aces and picture cards! No wonder he was winning and taking our money.

1947 was a memorable year for me. I was nine and discovered my second best hobby that year, and even today I am as keen as ever in this wonderful interest: Astronomy.

It was winter, and in the night sky due North in the constellation of Ursa Major (the plough to the ignorant) was a comet. Its name I believe was comet Bester. Named after its discoverer. It was in view to the naked eye for over a week until it was lost from sight as it approached the sun. Then only telescopes would be able to see it. I didn't have a telescope in those days, but have had several since. Including an eight-inch reflector whose lens I grinded myself (I now possess a telescope that is computer controlled).

Yet 1947 is remembered not for the comet, but the big, big freeze. It snowed for days on end, and then froze solid. Then it snowed again. For how long this continued I can't remember. I remember though the mountains of snow. If my memory is correct without exaggerating, I believe that we could have walked into our living room through the window, and this window was at least four foot off the ground. In the streets it kept piling up and up. Misery I expect for the whole country, but not for us kids. With balaclavas on, and socks for gloves we had a field day. Tunnels were dug and one could walk from one place to another without seeing the sky. The penalty for all this was the hot aches! It was shear murder when you got this, but you got no sympathy from grown-ups. It was a self-inflicted injury.

After months of this snow and freezing came another disaster, the thaw. Whole regions were flooded throughout the land. In Nottingham, the Meadows area was hit worst of all. This low-lying part of Nottingham had water in some places over eight feet high. I can remember seeing the water lapping up near Midland's station. A few days later it rose higher and rushed down Carrington Street. Yet there was fun for some even with this tragedy. Older boys than myself, ripped paling off from fences, some had brought home-made boats, whilst others used dustbins as boats and the palings as paddles.

I was getting older now, old enough to join the boys brigade. So I joined "Dako" on Dakeyne Street at the bottom of Carlton Road. The skipper was called Scotty I believe. I lasted just thirty minutes at Dako before being banned for life.

What was the hideous crime I had committed? I was on the stage, and on the floor about three feet below was the boy's brigade's huge big bass drum. This drum when they marched and paraded through the streets was thumped by a member wearing a leopard skin top. It was lying flat, making I thought, a good trampoline. So off the stage I jumped. I wasn't very heavy but I went clean through bursting the expensive drum skin. My feet didn't touch the ground as skipper grabbed me by an ear and frog marched me out of the hall and out of the boys brigade forever.

Not to be outdone I then joined the Russel Boys Club. Again at the bottom of Carlton Road in an old church building of some kind. Mr Potts was in charge, a good man. There I learned the skills of table tennis, snooker and billiards. I must have been a good lad from then on because I was still in this club up until my late teens.

Yet even this long spell in the Russel Boys Club ended in many of us getting kicked out. One weekend we travelled to a place called Western House. A good way off, though I don't know to this day whereabouts it was. Other clubs were there as well. The rules were strict. No visits to the country pub. No going to the girl's dormitory at any time etc.

You guessed it! I got kicked out of the club.

I have progressed too far and return back to earlier school days. Unlike today, we never really mixed with girls. Pierrepont Girls' School was near to Manvers, my school. So at finishing time hundreds of lads and lasses wend their way home. But the girls walked on one side of the road and the boys on the other. It would be considered being a sissy if you fraternised with the opposite sex. How different it is nowadays. Still on this subject, we were in the gym one day, I would be about fourteen to fifteen years of age. Eric Millar was telling us where and how babies were made. Most of us listening just couldn't believe him. That's a fact. Yes in those days we were very ignorant of things like that, and it did us no harm not to know as far as I am concerned. Our youth was spent on boy's stuff as described in these writings. Plenty of time for the other in later life.

Train spotting was a lot better than girl's stuff, every night saw me at Victoria Railway Station. Waiting for the five past nine Master Cutler express from London to Sheffield. A "namer" always pulled the Pullman coaches. Sometimes it would be the Flying Scotsman. Once this train had arrived I used to run like hell down Union Road to get home as fast as I could. Mum didn't know I was at this station.

However, one night my brother leaving night school spotted me legging it home. He snitched on me, getting me a clip round the ear. But I still went.

We come to the end of my boyhood memoirs. Just 1953 to deal with. Coronation year, and also the year I left school. Aunt Ada was the only one to have a TV in the family. So early on that day we all went to Aunties. Until late evening we sat in a packed room watching this event on a small nine inch black and white TV. All the streets were festooned with decorations, flags, and buntings etc. I remember making a coronation coach that was on the back of a Kellogg's corn flake box. Strange isn't it that today I have no interest in the royal family. I think they are all parasites, and the monarchy should be abolished.

My childhood was for me a truly happy time in my life. I had good parents, and my father was the salt of the earth. A smashing dad.

If I was told that I could win the jackpot on the lottery tomorrow but in doing so my childhood memories would be erased, then I would say: Stuff your jackpot, leave my memories be.

For they are good ones.

End

Other titles available from LOAF ON A STICK PRESS:

NOTTINGHAM RISING

The Great Cheese Riot of 1766 & the 1831 Reform Riots

By VALENTINE YARNSPINNER, Nottingham 2014

With this book, we have re-published our popular pamphlets, *To the Castle!...* and *Damn his Charity...*, together for the first time in a handsome paperback edition.

Damn his charity: In 1766 a riot broke out during Nottingham's Goose Fair. Large cheeses were snatched and rolled down Wheeler Gate and Peck Lane, apparently bowling over the mayor. The first part of this book looks into the story behind this tale and places the Great Cheese Riot within the context of the wave of Food Riots which took place that autumn.

To the Castle!: In October 1831 Nottingham Castle was burned down during the Reform Riots. Although this event is often referred to, little is known about who the rioters were and what may have motivated them. We took a close look at the direct action of these 'misguided rascals' and discuss their identities, motives as well as living and working conditions in early nineteenth century Nottingham.

ISBN 9780956913968, Paperback, 172 pages

£6 **www.peopleshistreh.wordpress.com**

A CITY OF LIGHT

Socialism, Chartism and Co-operation Nottingham 1844

By CHRISTOPHER RICHARDSON, Nottingham, 2nd edition 2015

In the dark days of the 1840s when Britain was hit by industrial stagnation, financial markets collapsed, and in Ireland famine stalked the land, working class pioneers sought new lives and futures, a new society of their own choosing – 'a city of light upon a hill'. They were not alone.

From the claustrophobic yards of the parish of St Mary and the gloomy streets of Narrow Marsh they came, courageous women and men seeking enlightenment from libraries that were theirs, from books and newspapers of their own choice, asserting the right to freedom of association. As chartists, socialists, co-operators, they challenged the inhumanities of the Poor Law; contested charges of sedition, blasphemy and riot; confronted the forces of established religion; and championed new forms of democratic control. Their struggles became beacons of hope.

These are stories from Nottingham in 1844, many of them previously untold, and their deeds resonate across the generations to this day.

ISBN 9780956913982, Paperback, 257 pages

£8 **www.acityoflight.wordpress.com**